"*Gettin' (un)Busy* is your to a calm, confident futu. "success equals busyness" myth and provides a blueprint for achievement. Read this book and leave your harried, frenetic days behind and embrace a life of purpose."

—SKIP PRICHARD
President & CEO, OCLC, Inc.
WSJ Bestselling Author of *The Book of Mistakes:*
9 Secrets to Creating a Successful Future

"I've helped thousands of people discover the work that they love. In *Gettin' (un)Busy*, you'll discover how to make sure that you don't allow even work you love to overtake your life. If you've ever felt like your soul needs to catch up with your body, this is the book for you."

—DAN MILLER
New York Times bestselling author,
48 Days to the Work You Love

"I want you to be a soul on fire. But your soul can't ignite if your calendar is crowded. You need space in your life if you're going to discover your passion and give your life to it. Garland Vance has crafted a masterful how-to book that helps you beat busyness and ignite your soul on fire."

—KARY OBERBRUNNER
author of *Day Job to Dream Job* and *Elixir Project*

"This book is essential reading for leaders who purpose to have a lifelong growth mindset. I've known Garland since before he was (un)busy, and I can tell you the transformation in his life—and the same transformation you'll experience if you follow these steps. You will stress less, grow more, and become a better steward of your life calling."

—JOHN D. BASIE, Ph.D.
Director, Masters Experience at Impact 360 Institute
Author of *Your College Launch Story:*
Six Things Every Parent Must Do

"Garland is one of the best I've ever worked with at helping leaders take complex ideas and making them easy to both understand and achieve. Follow his five steps, and you'll accomplish more while doing less."

—JOHN TORRES
Senior Vice President, Staff Support Learning Executive,
Bank of America

"When Garland started consulting with us at SafeHouse, our teamwork and focus was muddied with too many 'priorities.' We were exhausted and too overwhelmed to build a healthy work culture. Garland helped us discover how busyness was hurting us and how to get true clarity on our mission. Because of Garland's insights, our culture and mission are strong and clear and those whom we serve are resourced better because of it. There is no doubt in my mind that your team would benefit from Garland's passion and ability to communicate his insights."

—JOSH M. BRAY
CEO, SafeHouse Outreach, Atlanta, Georgia

"Feeling overwhelmed is one of those things that too many of us have resolved to live with for the rest of our lives. But who among us is intentionally setting out to always feel busy? If you truly want to create the life you want then you need to learn how to combat busyness in a healthy and sustainable way. This book is a manual for ridding your life of busyness, tapping into your purpose, learning true productivity and creating a greater sense of peace."

—MATTHEW BIVENS
Balance Lifestyle Coach
host of the *Having It A.L.L.* Podcast

"Everywhere I go, I hear people talk about how busy they are as if it's a badge of honor that somehow heightens their identity. With counter-cultural insight, Garland exposes the lie of busyness. He paints a picture of a better, more meaningful life that lies beyond the deception of busyness. And he shows you how easy it can be to redefine your life by gettin' (un)busy."

—DR. CRAIG CARR
Vice President for Administration for the Washington
Conference of Seventh-day Adventists

"When we greet family, friends and even strangers we ask, 'How are you?' What's their usual response? 'Busy!' We wear busyness like a badge of honor. But when busyness becomes stress and burnout, it feels less like honor and more like kryptonite. Our superpowers elude us. Our life purpose escapes us. In *Gettin' (un)Busy*, Garland Vance gives you five proven steps to break free from the trap of busyness and begin pursuing your dreams again."

—LINDA OUTKA
Leadership Coach,
Founder of Breakthrough Solutions, Inc.
Author of *Pebbles in My Shoe: Three Steps to Breaking through Interpersonal Conflict*

"Busy is the new lazy, and in this book Garland Vance provides a practical roadmap that will set you free to thrive without sacrificing the margin you need to enjoy life along the way."

—STEVE MOORE
President, nexleader
author of *Grow Toward Your Dreams: Practical Steps to Discover, Optimize and Unleash Your Potential*

"Garland provides an extremely thoughtful approach in his book, *Gettin' (un)Busy*. His writing, mixed with stories, insight, and evidence, will not only hold your attention, but also convince you that beating busyness is a real possibility no matter how busy you think you are. One read was not enough for me; I wanted to commit sections to memory so that I could better put them into practice. Leaders looking to be more productive in today's culture, which prioritizes busyness, will want to take a moment and learn from Garland and his (un)busy method."

—BENJAMIN F. MILLER, PsyD
Chief Strategy Officer, Well Being Trust

Garland Vance

GETTIN'
(un) BUSY

5 Steps to **Kill Busyness**
———— and Live with ————
Purpose, Productivity, and Peace

AUTHOR elite
ACADEMY

Published by Author Academy Elite
P.O. Box 43, Powell, OH 43065
www.AuthorAcademyElite.com

Library of Congress Cataloging 2018968546

Paperback: 978-1-64085-531-1
Hardback: 978-1-64085-532-8
E-book: 978-1-64085-533-5

Available in hardcover, paperback, e-book, and audiobook

For Dorothy, *the delight of my life.*
It has been more than trillium.

CONTENTS

FOREWORD: SCOTT WOZNIAK

Learning the principles in this book changed my life. They are not just theories. They are truths that work—drawn from understanding reality and working in harmony with the way the world is designed, not against it.

Garland has transformed his own life. He's been walking the talk for years. But he didn't start out as a world expert in productivity and wise living. When I first met Garland, more than 20 years ago, we were both counselors at one of the largest summer camps in the world. We weren't thinking about productivity in formal terms. We wanted to go big and seize the day. We were young, full of dreams and energy. We were the guys who got up earlier, worked harder, and tried to do it all.

For a while, it looked like that was the right approach to life. We both went on to more professional jobs, got married, got master's degrees (Garland even got a doctorate); we took on major leadership roles, had kids, and even did extra speaking and writing on the side.

But reality doesn't go away, even when you're ignoring it. You can burn the candle at both ends for a while. Eventually, though, you start to run out of wax. We both certainly did. We both experienced a physical crash. We suffered from "too many good things."

Thankfully for me, when I got to this place, Garland was a step ahead of me. And as I tried to figure out how to manage a life filled with too many good things, he stepped in to help. He didn't just encourage me, he opened his life and showedme how to actually make the changes. These principles are the real deal.

Grinding harder doesn't get better results in the long run. I've lived both ways and I will never go back. I can't wait for you to make it to the other side, too. Don't wait until you hit your wall. Read this book and start changing now.

Scott
WOZNIAK

CEO of Swoz Leadership & Author of *How to Fail as a Leader*
www.ScottWozniak.com

GETTIN' STARTED

"I'd love to stop being so busy...but I'm too busy to slow down." People have told me this with tongue-in-cheek hundreds of times.

But every time I've heard it, I knew there was a kernel of truth. Ever since I started writing this book, one thought has plagued me: *busy people don't have much time to read.*

I kept this complication in mind while writing *Gettin' (un)Busy.* My first draft was twenty-two thousand more words. I realized the extra fifty pages was too much for busy people. I kept it short to avoid overwhelming you but long enough to introduce the ideas and tools necessary for killing busyness.

In order to help you stay focused, I created *The 30-Day Gettin' (un)Busy Plan.*

This worksheet guides you daily through the pages to read and actions to take. Twenty-seven of the days involve reading less than ten pages. I also provided four days to catch up or take a break.

Download *The 30-Day Gettin' (un)Busy Plan* at **www. gettinunbusybook.com/tools**.

INTRODUCTION

*I feel like I'm drowning. I am overwhelmed at work and home.
I have so much to do, and I feel like I can't keep up with it all.*

Oliver said these words to me over coffee. As he spoke, he
dropped his head in shame and scanned the room to see if
anyone could hear him.

I met Oliver the day before at a productivity workshop I
was leading. He approached me at the conclusion of the day
and asked if I could help him customize his time management
solutions. The next morning, we sat at the hotel coffee shop,
and I asked him to tell me his story.

Oliver shared that he was a senior leader at his company.
He had started working for the company right out of college
and quickly moved up the ladder. People took notice of Oliver's
high capacity and competence, so they increased his project
load and the number of his direct reports.

Oliver now ran a department of 300 employees and had
nine people reporting directly to him. His teams consistently
achieved the best results of any team in the organization, and
people knew it was because of Oliver's leadership.

Oliver's team liked him. He cared about them and treated
them well, but he pushed them to do more than they thought
possible. His team was feeling a bit overwhelmed.

When I asked him about his family, Oliver told me that he and his wife, Sarah, had been married for fifteen years. They had two kids, an eight-year-old girl, and a five-year-old boy. "How do you feel when you go home?" I asked him.

He said he was rarely at home. I furrowed my brow in concern. Then he clarified that his whole family was rarely at home. Between the two kids, they spent most nights at basketball or soccer practice. There was also drama, ballet, horseback riding, piano lessons, and karate. He explained that when he was growing up, his parents only had enough money for him to play basketball and take piano lessons. He wanted to give his kids all the activities they wanted since he never got that.

I asked him if there were any other commitments he had. He told me he was on the board of a local homeless shelter which included monthly meetings and frequent opportunities to serve at the soup kitchen.

He also volunteered much of his time to his church. His wife was part of a weekly women's Bible study and served in the children's ministry, and they hosted a family group in their house every week.

When he got home most nights, Oliver said goodnight to his kids before they went to bed and then spent time catching up on email.

"When I'm home, I feel guilty for not being at work, and when I stay late to work, I feel guilty for not being at home."

He paused to fiddle with his wedding ring, then continued. "Do you want to know the irony of it all? I started reading more and more about time management this year to try to get a grip on this. I've gotten to know so much about it that our company's Chief Learning Officer asked me to teach a day-long workshop on time management!" With a look of defeat, Oliver paused, picked up his coffee mug and took a sip.

I leaned in, giving him a moment to swallow. It wasn't the first time I had heard a story like Oliver's. His story was familiar enough that I may have been able to tell it for him.

I thought I knew what his problem was, but I wanted to see if Oliver knew it.

"Oliver," I said, "it sounds like you've got a lot going on at work and home. What do you believe is the central problem you're trying to solve?"

Oliver said, "I can't accomplish everything I need to do. I have so many good things I want to do. I need to figure out how to get more done in less time. Can you help me with that?"

I took a sip of my coffee and then asked, "To be clear, you think the problem is your capacity? You think that you need to achieve more when you're awake? Maybe you should discipline yourself to stay awake more hours every day?"

He nodded.

"Oliver, you are already accomplishing a substantial amount of work. That's impressive. But I have one more question for you. How are you *feeling* amid all this accomplishment? How do you feel when you go to bed at night?"

That's when he said it. "I feel like I'm drowning. I am overwhelmed at work and home. I have so much to do that I feel like I can't keep up with it."

Oliver's commitments had exceeded his capacity.

Have you ever felt like Oliver?

- You fill your life with good commitments, but you feel stressed, exhausted, and overwhelmed.

- You wake up and go to bed exhausted.

- Your heart races at least once every day because you feel like you can't keep up.

- You feel like you're drowning but don't want others to know about it.

- You're afraid people won't respect you if you tell them you can't do it all.

Maybe, like Oliver, you've concluded the best way to alleviate these feelings is to increase your capacity. You convince yourself to learn better time management skills and get less sleep.

"Oliver," I told him, "your problem is not that you need better time management."

He looked stunned and a little disappointed.

I continued. "Don't get me wrong. I love time management, and I think it's beneficial. But you don't need more time management strategies."

His eyebrows raised in curiosity.

"If the problem is having too much *to do*, the solution cannot be to *do more*. Time management is not your problem."

He shoved aside his now empty coffee mug and leaned in. "But I came to you because I thought I had a time management issue. How is this not about time management?"

"Your dilemma is that you have too much to do. Yet you came to me expecting that I would give you *more*. Let me say it again. If you already have too much to do, you don't need more to do."

His eyes widened, and I could see the lightbulb flicker on. "You're right!"

"Oliver, your problem is busyness."

He looked puzzled. "Busyness?"

"Yes, busyness. If you don't kill busyness, it will kill you."

"That seems a little extreme. Why do you say that?"

"Because it almost killed me."

BLUEPRINT FOR
(UN)BUSYNESS

I am concerned for your life.
If you don't kill busyness, it will kill you.
I am concerned for your life.
The same way my doctor was concerned for mine.

1

MY TERMINAL DIAGNOSIS

During my annual checkup, Dr. Tate looked me in the eye, put his hand on my shoulder and said the words I am saying to you now.

"I am concerned for your life."

I had shared with Dr. Tate that I was experiencing four strange symptoms.

First, I was exhausted. All the time. I would go to bed exhausted and wake up exhausted. No matter what I did or how much sleep I got, I felt exhausted.

Second, my heart would race multiple times every day. I would pour sweat and have difficulty breathing. These spells weren't occurring during strenuous activity. They happened while I checked email, had dinner or watched TV.

Third, I experienced forgetfulness. I told Dr. Tate, "My wife, Dorothy, and I will have a conversation one night and come to an important decision. The next morning, she will reference the conversation, and I'll have no idea what she's talking about."

Dr. Tate chuckled. "That may just be called 'being a man.'"

Fourth, I was having chronic, debilitating migraines three times every week. They started in my shoulders, moved up the base of my neck and worked their way around my whole head. It felt like a giant eagle gripping its talons into my skull

3

and eyes. All I could do was turn out all the lights, lay down, and try to sleep.

Dr. Tate expressed concern over these four symptoms, but he wanted to dig deeper before a diagnosis. "Tell me about your commitments and what your life looks like."

"I'm busy," I told him, "but it's a good busy."

"What do you mean by busy?"

"I work between fifty to sixty hours per week in a job that I love. I direct a division of a large nonprofit, training college students in leadership development. I am responsible for a small staff. Because I work with college students, I stay up late. The earliest I get to bed is midnight, though it's often later.

"I'm also earning my doctorate in leadership, which means that I'm up early—usually between 4:30 or 5:00 am—to study before my kids get up.

"Between school and work, I travel about sixty days per year.

"I have an incredible family. Dorothy and I have three great kids, but they're young and still require a lot of vigilance and attention. We've intentionally limited the number of activities they do. Each one gets to pick one extracurricular activity. But because of my work and school schedule, I don't get to spend the quality time with them that I want.

"Dorothy and I are involved with developing the leadership of our church. These are people who we deeply love and who get a lot of our time.

Dr. Tate said, "Wow, Garland. That sounds like a lot. Is there anything else?"

"Yes. We've had to slow down a lot over the last year."

Dr. Tate's eyes widened. "You've slowed down?"

"My mom passed away last year after a nine-month battle with cancer. We've slowed down this year to give ourselves time and space to heal."

Dr. Tate asked, "How are you dealing with the death of your mom?"

"I'm doing okay. I miss her a lot, but I think I'm grieving well. About a month after she died, I identified six goals for healthy grieving. In the last year, I've accomplished five of the six, and I'm on my way to complete the sixth one.

At that moment, Dr. Tate put his hand on my shoulder and said the words that changed my life. "Garland, I am concerned for your life."

He kept going. "I think I know what your problem is. You are stressed out."

It took a minute for those words to sink in. He had told me he was "concerned for my life." I was expecting a terminal illness. Instead, he diagnosed me with something as benign and commonplace as stress?

I got irritated. I kept thinking, *stress is something that incompetent people have. Stress is for those who aren't smart enough to manage their time.*

With frustration brimming, I said, "Dr. Tate, I've just described four symptoms that are raising serious concerns for me, including uncontrollable migraines. Now you're telling me that the cause of all these symptoms is stress? *I don't feel stressed!*"

With a smile on his face, he said, "But your head does."

I continued. "I love my life. I like every part of it: my family, job, school, friends, and church. Why do you think I'm stressed?"

He responded, "Because you're busy."

I retorted, "I know I'm busy. It's a good busy. Besides, everyone is busy."

"You're right. Everyone's busy. And it's killing us all."

After my diagnosis, I decided I needed to get (un)busy before busyness killed me. I didn't know where to begin. Since I was earning a Doctorate in Leadership and Spiritual Formation, I decided to focus my studies. I started reading more about busyness. I read about busyness from multiple perspectives—physical, spiritual, psychological, and practical. I researched time management and minimalism. I investigated the effects of stress and busyness on leaders. I studied how leaders can beat busyness while simultaneously increasing their impact and results.

I didn't want to stop at *studying* busyness. I wanted to apply it to my own life. I desired to help my friends and family and co-workers and neighbors beat busyness.

In all my research, though, I was continually disappointed. Many authors could tell me the problems that came from busyness. Some of them could tell me a few best practices that would cut down on busyness. But no one could tell me a process for beating busyness while remaining highly productive. So, I decided to make it my mission to develop a step-by-step solution for beating busyness. This topic ended up being the focus of my dissertation.

That's why I'm glad you're reading this book. I am concerned for your life. You're busy, and it's probably a "good busy." But if you don't kill busyness, it will kill you.

2
BUSYNESS AS A BADGE OF HONOR

Everywhere I look I see busy people. On a recent vacation to Virginia, I needed a laundromat. The cashier greeted me, and I asked how he was doing.

He responded, "I'm good. Busy, though. You know, really busy. But I'm good."

Everyone is busy. At least it seems that way. Ask any of your friends how they're doing, and they're likely to tell you they're busy. From CEO's to stay-at-home parents, they're all busy. From high school students to retired couples, they're busy.

Everyone seems too busy. The chances are good that you're overcommitted and busy (or you wouldn't have picked up this book).

But overcommitment was not the expectation for our generation. In 1967, futurist Herman Kahn predicted that by the year 2000 the average person would need to work only thirty hours per week and have thirteen weeks of vacation due to the increases in technology and wages.[1]

Has that been your experience? Most people have a very different experience than what Kahn predicted.

- According to the US Travel Association, the average number of vacation days has dropped from twenty-one days in 2000 to sixteen days in 2013.

- At the same time, the number of hours people work has gone up. According to a Gallup survey in August 2014:

  Adults employed full time in the U.S. report working an average of 47 hours per week, almost a full workday longer than what a standard five-day, 9-to-5 schedule entails. In fact, half of all full-time workers indicate they typically work more than 40 hours, and nearly four in ten say they work at least 50 hours.[2]

- A Putman study from 2000 indicates that the number of people who "always feel rushed" increased 50% between 1960 and 1990. (Has your pace of life increased since 1990?)

- In 2005, the National Institute for Occupational Safety and Health found that "40% of all workers today feel overworked, pressured, and squeezed to the point of anxiety, depression, and disease."[3]

- In Japan, "death by overworking" has become so prevalent that they have a term for it, *karoshi*. Recent statistics report that almost 1,500 Japanese workers have died from *karoshi*. There is even a secretary general of the National Defense Counsel for Victims of Karoshi named Hiroshi Kawahito who believes that the actual figures could be ten times higher.

Busyness isn't only affecting your work life. It's also infecting your home:

- Americans often experience a common illness known as "leisure sickness."[4] The flu-like symptoms include a

8

headache, sore throat, and muscle aches. Leisure sickness occurs during evenings, weekends, and vacations when a person slows down. Their bodies are so stressed out and worn out that they break down.

- Adults also spend more time doing "informal work."[5] The Bureau of Labor Statistics reported in 2015 that parents of young children spend seven hours every workday taking care of their kids. "Earlier generations gave children more independence and mobility, but today's parenting is more time and labor intensive."[6]

- According to *Psychology Today* in 2008, "The average high school kid today has the same level of anxiety as the average psychiatric patient in the early 1950's. We are getting more anxious every decade."[7] Some of the leading causes of anxiety for teenagers are overcommitment and putting too much pressure on themselves to perform all of their commitments with excellence. (Both *The Atlantic*[8] and *The Washington Post*[9] have recorded that anxiety levels have continued to rise since the publication of *Psychology Today's* article.)

Busyness has become so prevalent that the authors of *The 5 Choices* say, "Busyness is the existential claim of the 21st century. *I am stressed out. Therefore, I am.*"[10]

Busyness has become more than a condition of your calendar. You treat it like a condition of your character. You wear your busyness like a badge of honor. It makes you feel alive because you're doing good things. It makes you feel significant because (un)busy people must not be very important.

You frantically and frenetically move through each day. You rush from one commitment to the next, from one meeting to the next, and from one obligation to the next.

You wake up exhausted and go to bed exhausted. You don't have time to celebrate significant accomplishments because you have another commitment. You need to schedule six weeks in advance to grab lunch with your best friend because both of your calendars are full.

You go through your day feeling stressed, overwhelmed and exhausted. When you can't do all the things you think you need to do, you convince yourself that, like Oliver, you need better time management skills, to sleep less, or to work an extra hour at night.

You don't have enough time to figure out what your biggest dreams and highest priorities are because you're busy "doing" life.

Still, you wear busyness like a badge of honor. "I am busy. Therefore, I am."

It's not only crazy, it's psychotic.

After I began my research on busyness, I saw it everywhere. Then one day at church, my wife, Dorothy, saw an acquaintance. Dorothy greeted her and asked how she was doing.

She replied, "I'm good. Just busy… *psychotically* busy. But it's a good busy, you know?"

When Dorothy told me about the conversation, we marveled together: *Why is something that drives you to psychosis a good thing?*

My first goal in this book is to convince you that busyness is not a good thing. It's killing you. It's robbing you of your quantity and quality of life. It's destroying your productivity and your leadership. And it's wrecking entire organizations. Busyness is a terrible thing, yet we think it's good.

WHY WE THINK BUSYNESS IS GOOD

Everyone is busy. People boast about busyness, telling random strangers in the laundromat about it. If busyness is something so many people proclaim, it must mean busyness is a good thing, right? No one brags about something they think is bad.

However, busyness is not a good thing. It is nothing to boast about and nothing we should claim with pride.

Why have we all assumed that busyness is a good thing? Because our good commitments built our busyness.

Busyness is an overcommitment to too many good commitments.

When I was busy, my life was full of *good* commitments. Work, family, school, church, friendships—all of these were good. But when I added those good commitments together, they became too much. They became the opposite of good. They became bad.

I've had conversations about busyness with thousands of people. In all that time, I've never met anyone who was busy because they had committed to too many bad activities. Granted, I'm sure some evil dictators are busy. Some drug dealers may be busy, but I don't typically hang out with them. Every busy person I've ever met was busy because of an overcommitment to *good* commitments.

Too many good commitments add up to a bad life.

A few years ago, my family went out for sushi. My oldest son ordered the Scorpion Roll. It was massive—two rolls in one. Usually, he would split the Scorpion Roll with his sister, but she wasn't with us. My son finished the entire plate by himself. For the next few years, if anyone said the word *sushi* around him, he would turn green and feel sick to his stomach.

Sushi is good. Really good. The Scorpion Roll is good, but he ate so much of a good thing that it became bad. The same is true with busyness. You can add so many good commitments to your life that it becomes bad.

Busyness is an overcommitment to too many good commitments.

How Good Commitments Become Bad

How do these good commitments become bad? Before I answer that, I'd like you to answer a few questions.

- What do you want from your life?

- What are your biggest dreams and highest priorities?

- Do you have the time, energy, and attention to consistently and intentionally move toward those biggest dreams and highest priorities?

Before you move on, think about these questions for three minutes. Jot down some of your answers.

I've asked hundreds of people those questions, and I've found a trend. First, people get excited when they talk about what they want from life. Those I've surveyed have dreams for their families, future adventures, businesses, and giving to others. But when I've asked the third question about their time, energy, and attention, they shake their heads with regret. People don't have the time, energy, and attention to bring their dreams into reality, to live the life they want to live.

How do your good commitments become bad? Your good commitments distract you. They distract you from:

- discovering and living out your purpose

- realizing your biggest dreams

- accomplishing your highest priorities

- engaging the most significant people in your life

- living the life that you want and are meant to live

Busyness sacrifices your passions and priorities on the altar of good commitments. You give up the quantity and quality of your life to give your time, energy, and attention to good things that you feel obligated to do rather than the great things that you long to do. In exchange, you're loaded down with stress, overwhelm, and exhaustion.

I've seen this happen in friends, clients, and even entire organizations. I've seen CEO's whose calendars are so full of good commitments that they can't lead their organizations to accomplish their goals. I've seen it in stay-at-home parents who pack their kids' schedules so tight the family doesn't have time to be together. I've seen it in college students who fill their afternoons and evenings with clubs, work, and activities but graduate from college having missed the great experience. I've seen it in pastors who offer so many church programs that their congregation begins to resent spending time at church.

That's why I am concerned for your life.
Busyness will suck the life out of you.
You will become a shell of the person you wanted to be.
You will sacrifice your biggest dreams and highest priorities.

I am concerned for your life.
If you don't kill busyness, it will kill you.

3

THE BLUEPRINT FOR GETTIN'
(UN)BUSY

B
y this point, maybe you're convinced busyness isn't good. (Don't worry if you're not; you will be by the end of Chapter 4.)

I hear what you're thinking. It's a question that's been asked of me dozens of time. "Okay, Garland, you've convinced me busyness isn't good, but, if I'm not busy, what will I do?"

There's a bigger question that lies beneath that one. I think the real statement you're making is, "Garland, I want to live a significant life. I want to realize my dreams, have a great family, do meaningful work, and have a significant impact on the world. Busyness has been my attempt to do that. If I'm not busy, then *who will I be?*"

I'm convinced this desire to be significant drives much of your busyness. You want to live a big, meaningful, purposeful life that impacts and influences people.

I had the same desires when Dr. Tate diagnosed my problem. I wanted to live a big, meaningful, purposeful life that impacted and influenced people. I had even discovered and articulated my life purpose. In the process, though, I had convinced myself that impact and influence necessitate busyness.

Have you convinced yourself that influential people are busy? That overcommitment is evidence of one's significance?

Do you determine your importance by your number of projects and priorities? Have you convinced yourself that the busier you are, the more important you are?

I had myself believing the same things, but, in the process, I crammed my life so full of busyness that I diminished my **Purpose, Productivity, and Peace**.

Purpose, Productivity, and Peace

When you get (un)busy, what do you get in exchange? You get a life filled with Purpose, Productivity, and Peace.

Purpose is knowing your *why*. Your *why* is the reason you're on the planet. It's what you have to contribute to the world. Your purpose is the lasting mark you're going to leave generations after you're gone.

Purpose is the overarching *why* that gives reason to your actions.

Productivity is doing your *why*. Productivity isn't about getting more done or getting things done faster. It's not about filling your life and calendar and task list with all the things you need to do.

Productivity is about working to advance your *why*. If you know your *why*, it guides your actions. Productivity is about waking up every morning with clarity about what needs to happen to move your purpose forward. It's about going to bed every evening knowing that you've done what you committed to do.

Lots of busy people know their *why*. I did. Dorothy and I had trained hundreds of people to discover and articulate their purpose.

Lots of busy people have even taken steps toward fulfilling their *why*. I certainly had, but when you get (un)busy, you get the third, most often lost benefit—**peace**.

Peace is about resting in your *why*. Peace is a sense of calmness and confidence that comes from knowing, *I can do anything I want, but I can't do everything at once.*

You experience peace when you realize you have limited time, energy, and attention, so you selectively choose actions to advance your purpose. Peace comes when you live at a pace of life that allows you to take productive steps toward your purpose without exhausting yourself.

I didn't experience peace until I killed busyness.

Most people try to cram purpose and productivity into unpeaceful lives. You may have discovered your purpose and enhanced your productivity, but you squeeze it into an overcrowded life.

I've become convinced if you want a life of Purpose, Productivity and Peace, you must start with Peace. You enhance purpose and productivity by extinguishing stress, overwhelm, and exhaustion. I wrote this book so you can get Peace.

THE 5 STEPS TO GETTIN' (UN)BUSY

It took me years of research, interviews, and conversations, as well as personal trial and error, to discover how to get (un) busy so that I could live with Purpose, Productivity, and Peace. However, one of the greatest insights came from a television rerun I saw while I was working on my doctoral dissertation.

In 2003, NBC's *The Today Show* featured Lloyd, a man from Los Angeles, who had collected 5,000 bike parts—in one room of his house! Lloyd was a hoarder, a mental health condition that affects approximately 14 million people in the United States alone.

Lloyd was in his twenties when he lost his job as a computer programmer. Without any income, he saw bicycles people were throwing out. He believed he could save the bikes, so he started collecting them, hoping one day to repair them.

Unfortunately, Lloyd's appetite for collecting outweighed the time he had to repair. One single room was filled up with over 5,000 bike parts. Eventually, the rest of his house filled up as well. Lloyd could not get through the front of his home, so he slept outside—for twenty years.

Lloyd's condition didn't affect only his life. He lost friends and became alienated from his family. His neighbors resented him because of his expanding house of junk.

A judge finally issued a threat to Lloyd: either clean up his house or go to jail. The judge made Lloyd trim down his collection from 5,000 parts to fifteen bikes. It took a crew of 120 people a full month and 1,500 hours to clean out his house.

In recent years, hoarders like Lloyd have fascinated us. From television shows to documentaries to books, we gawk at hoarders. They are fascinating—or maybe the word I'm looking for is *psychotic*—just like us busy people.

Busyness is a form of hoarding.

- Hoarding is the compulsion to over-collect. Busyness is the compulsion to overcommit.

- Hoarders gather stuff. Busy people gather experiences.

- Hoarders refuse to purge items. Busy people refuse to purge activities.

As I researched busyness, I found myself drawn to stories about hoarding, struck by the similarities. I noticed that to change their habits, hoarders moved through a step-by-step process. We hoarders of commitments require a process as well.

In this book, I'll introduce you to the five steps of Gettin' (un)Busy. These steps move you from feeling stressed, overwhelmed, and exhausted to living and leading with Purpose, Productivity, and Peace.

Step 1: Decide. In the first step, you make three decisions. First, Decide if busyness is worth its effects. Second, Decide if you are busy. Third, Decide to get (un)busy. The remainder of the steps hinges on your decision to get (un)busy.

Step 2: Deconstruct. In the second step, you will Deconstruct false beliefs, bad habits, and (un)wanted commitments that trap you in busyness. You must Deconstruct these before you can build a life of Purpose, Productivity, and Peace.

Step 3: Design. During this step, you'll Design the life you want to live. You'll identify the pace at which you want to live. You will create space for four critical elements of living a life of Purpose, Productivity, and Peace: Relationships, Recreation, Rest, and Reflection. You'll design time to focus on your biggest dreams and highest priorities.

Step 4: Develop. In this step, you will see your life filled with Purpose, Productivity, and Peace as you implement new ways of living. You'll Develop an (un)busy calendar, (un)busy mind, and (un)busy habits that enable you to fulfill your biggest dreams and highest priorities.

Step 5: Draw Others In. Once you are living an (un)busy life, you will Draw in your family, friends, and coworkers to get (un)busy together so that you all can live with Purpose, Productivity, and Peace.

Get (un)busy before busyness kills you. Let's get started with the first step.

STEP 1

DECIDE

Busyness has become both normal and expected. It's normal because everyone talks about how busy they are. It's expected because people believe that they should be busy—or at least say they are.

Because busyness is normal and expected, Gettin' (un)Busy is abnormal and unexpected! That's why the first step is to Decide. You must decide to do something that is different from many people. Before you can eliminate busyness, you must first make three decisions.

1. Decide if busyness is worth it.

Through research and observations, you'll discover the effects busyness has on you. I'll show you how busyness is literally killing you and damaging your relationships. I'll also show you how it's destroying your productivity and its impact on entire organizations. You'll see the price you pay for busyness.

2. Decide if you are too busy.

If you picked up this book, the chances are high that you're busy. To help you know for sure, I'll share with you several indicators that you're too busy. Additionally, you can take a free online assessment that will help you decide if you're too busy.

3. Decide to get (un)busy.

Every act of courage begins with a decision. Just because you know what busyness is doing to you doesn't mean you'll choose to beat it. Before moving on to the next step, you must Decide to get (un)busy.

4

DECIDE IF BUSYNESS
IS WORTH IT

N ot too long ago, nearly everyone smoked; it was even believed to be healthy.[11] Then the Surgeon General announced smoking was killing people. Busyness is the same. It's been said that busyness is the new smoking.[12]

Busyness is killing you. I'm not exaggerating here. It's literally killing you. You must decide if busyness is worth it because it's taking a toll on you. In this chapter, you will learn the physical, mental, emotional, and relational effects of your overcommitment. I will also share the consequences on your productivity and on entire organizations.

PHYSICAL EFFECTS

In the 1980s there was a video that showed a hot frying pan. A narrator said, "This is drugs." Then an egg was cracked into the hot frying pan. The egg sizzled and burned. The narrator said, "This is your brain on drugs. Any questions?"

This commercial could be remade today, but the frying pan would be busyness instead of drugs.

Busyness is killing you physically. To understand how, you must understand stress and how your body is designed to work with it.

According to Dr. Hans Selye, the father of stress research, stress is "the nonspecific response of the body to any demand."[13] Your body encounters demands every single day. Stress by itself is not bad.

In fact, Selye differentiates between bad stress (called **Distress**) and good stress (called **Eustress**). Distress is caused by undesirable circumstances, such as getting into a car accident, having your boss call you into her office unexpectedly or running into a bear during a hike.

Eustress is caused by desirable circumstances, like watching the last minutes of a close football game or seeing your kid perform a solo in the school musical.

Distress is due to fear or anxiety. Eustress is stress due to excitement or anticipation. I feel eustress every time I speak publicly. I love public speaking. The bigger the crowd, the better I feel, but it's still stressful because I want to articulate my thoughts well. I want the audience to enjoy the speech and to like me.

Whenever you encounter stress, your body goes through a **Stress Cycle** comprised of five phases.

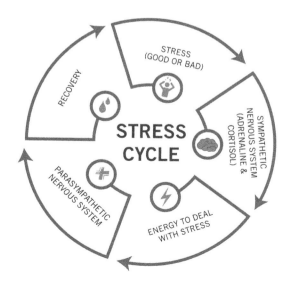

In the first phase, you encounter stress (either good or bad). Imagine that you're hiking and come across a bear in the woods. The moment you encounter this bear-induced stress, you experience the second phase: your body responds by using the **sympathetic nervous system**, which releases *adrenaline and cortisol.*

Adrenaline gives you the fight, flight, or freeze response. It focuses you to meet the demands of dealing with the bear. It floods you with energy to either fight the bear (not a good idea) or run from it.

Cortisol has several functions that help you deal with the bear.

- It shuts down unnecessary bodily systems to divert all your energy to deal with the bear. During a bear attack, you don't need your immune, digestive or reproductive systems to work.

- It increases your fear. If you don't have any fear, you'll end up as the bear's next meal.

- It focuses your motivation. When you see the bear, you immediately develop a motivation to stay alive. All other hopes and dreams get put to the side. You want to survive and hopefully come out unscathed.

- It affects your mood. You don't have the ability to be happy when you see the bear. Your mood becomes serious.

The release of adrenaline and cortisol cause you to enter the third phase: you have the energy to deal with the stress.

Now imagine that you fled from the bear. You've made it back to your car and have driven home. After a few hours, you'll begin the fourth phase: your **parasympathetic nervous** n **(PNS)** will kick in. You'll feel exhausted, like all your energy has been drained. You'll need to rest and recuperate.

In the final phase, the PNS helps you to recover from surges of adrenaline and cortisol and helps your heart rate slow down to normal. It restores your body to a state of calmness and gets you back to a state of equilibrium. It helps your body recuperate so you will be ready to encounter the next stressor (hopefully, not another bear encounter).

What does this little science lesson have to do with busyness? There are five insights:

1. Your body can't tell the difference between Eustress and Distress.

When your body encounters stress, your brain doesn't discern between good stress or bad stress. It simply experiences stress. Your mind doesn't know the difference between the stress of meeting a deadline for an important project and the stress of meeting a bear that wants to eat you.

2. Busyness introduces constant stress into your life.

Busyness is an overcommitment to too many good commitments. When you're overcommitted, your body can't tell the difference between meeting a bear or between having too many meetings at your office.

Busy people pack their days full and, therefore, need to rush. They must rush to get out the door to make it to work. They rush from one meeting to the next all day long. In spare moments between meetings, they rush to respond to email. They rush away from the office at the end of the day so that they can get home. They rush their kids around to all their activities. They rush to get dinner on the table. They rush to touch base with their partner.

All this rushing causes stress. Busy people constantly introduce stressors into their lives.

3. Every time you encounter stress, your sympathetic nervous system releases adrenaline and cortisol.

The release of adrenaline and cortisol has both positive and negative effects.

Positively, the adrenaline feels very good. It releases energy into your body so you can deal with the situation. However, the negative effects outweigh the positive:

- The cortisol shuts down other systems in your body. Your body stops functioning as it's designed.

- Cortisol increases your fear. Rather than feeling curious or bold, you release chemical anxiety into your body.

- Cortisol lowers your mood. You don't feel happy or enjoy life when you're operating out of fear.

- Cortisol focuses your motivation on what's directly in front of you. You can't think about long term dreams or aspirations because you are focused on the stress-causing challenge directly in front of you.

If you only encountered stress once or twice every day, these effects wouldn't be so bad. But busy people encounter stress dozens of times (or more) every day. Thus, you keep your body coursing with adrenaline and cortisol, which is worsened by the next effect.

4. Busyness short-circuits your parasympathetic nervous system.

Every time you encounter stress, your body needs time to recover, but busy people don't take time to recuperate. They rush from one commitment to the next. They schedule every minute of their days. Therefore, your parasympathetic nervous system never has time to recover before you introduce the next form of stress and short circuit your body's natural abilities. The next diagram illustrates the effect of busyness on the Stress Cycle.

BUSYNESS BLOCKS THE STRESS CYCLE

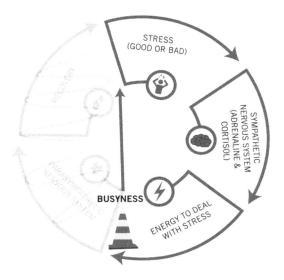

5. Short-circuiting your parasympathetic nervous system has destructive physical, mental, emotional, relational, productivity, and organizational effects.

Imagine what happens when:

- You regularly short-circuit your immune, digestive, and reproductive systems.

- You introduce stress and never give yourself time to recover.

- Your fear increases and your mood decreases.

- Your motives stay fixed on what's right in front of you rather than thinking about your long-term goals and aspirations.

Multiple doctors have documented the following effects of our overcommitted lives: diarrhea, prolonged fatigue, insomnia, lack of appetite, loss of libido, inability to concentrate, frequent illness, rapid or skipped heartbeat, depression, anxiety, chronic muscle tension, headaches, colitis, diverticulitis, ulcers, constipation, and loss of enthusiasm for life.[14]

In other words, all this eustress leads to distress.

This is your body on busyness. Any questions?

EMOTIONAL EFFECTS

Burnout has become a common word for our exhausted generation. We don't talk about merely being tired. We talk about being burned out. Because it's a common expression, it surprises many people when I tell them that burnout is an actual condition.

In 1986, Dr. Christina Maslach first wrote about burnout within helping professions like doctors, nurses or clergy. By 2003, she had identified burnout as being common among busy people.[15]

Burnout has three stages:

"In the first stage, *emotional exhaustion*, people feel drained and used up. Their emotional resources are depleted, and there is no source for replenishment. Individuals put distance between themselves and those whose needs and demands are overwhelming. In the second stage, *depersonalization*, individuals develop poor opinions of others and expect the worst from them, even actively disliking them. The third stage of burnout corresponds with a feeling of hopelessness that is the result of a *reduced sense of personal accomplishment*."[16]

Alex Soojung-Kim Pang expounds on some of the effects of these three stages:

31

"Workers suffering from burnout become detached from work, are less empathetic to colleagues and customers and feel that their work has little value to themselves or the world; it can also create marriage and family problems and contribute to depression, poor health, and – especially among formerly hard-charging and career-oriented people – higher rates of suicide."[17]

In my years of working with busy people, I've never had one person tell me they haven't experienced any of these three stages. Almost without exception, people can tell me exactly which stage of burnout they're experiencing.

By the time I met with Oliver, he knew he was in Stage 3. He said he felt drained of all energy and motivation (emotional exhaustion). He resented his wife, kids, and co-workers who needed his help (depersonalization). Oliver felt like a hamster running on a wheel—no matter how hard he worked or how much he did, he never accomplished anything significant (loss of sense of personal accomplishment).

What is busyness doing to you emotionally? It's leading to burnout. Burnout has a massive effect on your relationships.

Relational Effects

Busyness often happens because you care deeply about others. You want your kids to be happy and well-rounded, so you get them involved in multiple activities. You want your team at work and your company's shareholders to succeed, so you add more projects to get higher profit margins. You love your partner, so you plan more activities to do together. You adore your family so you commit to more home projects to improve your quality of life. You cherish your community, so you volunteer for multiple service opportunities.

Busyness often occurs because you love others so much. When you love them that much, it's easy to overcommit.

Unfortunately, the very act of giving your loved ones your time and energy can lead to depersonalization.

Depersonalization (the second stage of burnout) occurs when you have so much to do that you resent others. You get annoyed at interruptions. You groan when your kids need your help. You roll your eyes when your employee knocks on your office door.

The effects of depersonalization can be seen from an experiment. In 1970, Daniel Batson and John Darley worked with students at Princeton Theological Seminary to conduct an experiment using Jesus's fictional story of the Good Samaritan found in the New Testament. If you're not familiar with the Good Samaritan, here's the story.

A guy goes on a journey when, out of nowhere, a group of bandits beats, robs, and leaves him for dead. A little bit later, a priest comes walking by and sees the man. The priest doesn't want to deal with him, so he passes by on the other side of the road. A little later, a Levite (another religious guy) does the same thing.

Finally, a Samaritan sees the man. (In Jesus's day, a Samaritan was a type of person who would have been hated by Jesus's audience). The Samaritan sees the injured man and helps him. He takes him to a lodge, pays all his bills, and promises to return to pay for any other bills the man might incur.

Back to the experiment. The seminary students took a brief survey and then they were instructed to go to a different building across campus. Once at the new building, they would either discuss jobs that seminary graduates might be interested in or deliver a talk about Jesus's story of the Good Samaritan.

Before students left, each was given one of three scenarios:

1. They were already late and needed to get to the other building very quickly (high hurry).

2. They had just enough time to get to the other building if they hurried (medium hurry).

3. They had a few minutes before they needed to be at the next building and could take their time (low hurry).

Unknown to the participants, Darley and Batson put a twist in the experience. They arranged for a man to dress in rags and lie down on the sidewalk. As each participant approached, the man would cough two times, moan and appear to be in significant pain.

How did the seminary students respond? Of the seventy students who participated, 63% of those in low hurry helped the victim, 45% in medium hurry helped, but only 10% in high hurry assisted the man. Even the students who were supposed to deliver a talk on the Good Samaritan walked past, or in some cases, literally stepped over the victim!

In other words, the ministers-in-training who were on their way to deliver a talk on the Good Samaritan failed to act like one! They depersonalized the man.

Busyness leads to depersonalization. You stop seeing the people in your life as people. Instead, you see them as tools or obstacles. They are tools that can make your life easier or help you accomplish your goals or they're obstacles that interrupt your overcommitted life.

Depersonalization can lead you to "actively dislike" the people you love the most. You resent your spouse. You begrudge your kids. You stay frustrated with your team at work. Nothing destroys relationships as quickly as active dislike!

MENTAL EFFECTS

Have you ever been working on something important and suddenly remember you're supposed to pick up eggs on the way home? You stuff that thought into the back of your mind and get back to your work, but you keep remembering that you need to pick up eggs, even as you go into your next meeting.

Add to this scenario the typical busy person's schedule. You not only have to pick up eggs, you must finish your report for work, meet with your employee to review his performance, call your dad to wish him a happy birthday, and get to your daughter's soccer game on time.

So far, you've seen that busyness destroys your body, wrecks your emotions, and harms your relationships. I've got more bad news for you. It wreaks havoc on your mind with three ugly effects.

1. Busyness prevents you from focusing.

Busy people don't simply multi-task; they attempt to multi-focus. Almost nothing gets your full attention. Instead, your mind operates like a computer running twenty programs simultaneously. You may only look at one program, but all those other programs take up RAM and slow down the computer.

The same is true in your brain. You can't focus when you're busy because you have too many moving parts all shifting simultaneously. There are too many thoughts flying around your head.

You can't give your full attention to anything. You only give a small percentage of your attention to your most critical decisions, your most important priorities, your most pressing problems.

If you can't focus, you'll miss the trends in the market that warned you of the need to pivot. You'll miss the moment when your daughter scores the game-winning goal for her soccer team. You'll forget about stopping by the grocery store to pick up eggs.

2. Busyness distracts you from your highest priorities.

One of the distinctions that sets humans apart from apes is the executive functions of your brain. Executive functions are also one of the keys to success in life and work, giving you the ability to prioritize, evaluate, plan, accomplish, and adapt.

In every area of your life, you need to:

- decide what is most important (**Prioritize**);

- determine if you're doing what's most important (**Evaluate**);

- figure out how to do what's most important (**Plan**);

- do what's most important (**Accomplish**); and

- change course in the moment as more important opportunities present themselves (**Adapt**).

If you're going to live purposefully, you need to Prioritize, Evaluate, Plan, Accomplish and Adapt both personally and professionally. But busyness traps you in a state of constant urgency (remember the effects of cortisol?).

You're too busy to give time and attention to determine what's most important.

You have too many commitments to evaluate whether you're doing what's most important. You don't take time to plan and schedule your priorities. You certainly can't accomplish what you need to do.

Busyness even blinds you to unexpected opportunities that would have allowed you to live out your highest priorities.

3. Busyness inhibits reflection.

Reflection is one of the most important habits of a life well-lived. We'll talk more about this in Chapter 11 (The Core 4). Reflection gives you the ability to remember what has happened, to express gratitude for the good, and to answer critical questions like, "What went wrong? What could have prevented that negative outcome from happening? What could I do differently next time?"

Reflection isn't just about the past. It can help you Prioritize, Evaluate, Plan, Accomplish, and Adapt. Reflection enables you to think about the future:

- Are you headed in the right direction?

- If you continue doing what we're doing, what will the result be in the next five years?

- What do you want your life to look like in the next ten years?

Reflection has one other benefit. According to *Lead Yourself First: Inspiring Leadership through Solitude*, taking time for reflection in solitude can expand your courage. Courage to make the hard decisions emerges from solitude and reflection.[18]

Busyness convinces you that you must move forward constantly. It tells you: "There is always something else that needs to be done *now*. You don't have time to look back and reflect on what has already happened."

If you're too busy, you won't take the time to reflect on the past or future, and busyness will short-circuit your courage.

I experienced this a few years ago with a team I led. We needed to make some enormous changes, but I couldn't get clear on what we needed to do. I couldn't even get consensus that we needed to change. Even though I knew this was important, my calendar was too full. I was booked up with meetings weeks in advance. I was too busy.

Finally, I cleared my calendar for an entire day. I got out of the office and turned off all my devices. I took a pen and paper and spent the day at Starbucks. I journaled. I reflected on the challenges that our team was facing and on the reluctance of the team. I thought through how my leadership was harming the team. I thought through the strategy and priorities that needed to happen for change to take place.

By the end of the day, I could clearly articulate the problem and was convinced that a change needed to take place now. I also knew that it was my responsibility to lead the change, even if others didn't agree. Reflection led to both clarity and courage.

PRODUCTIVITY EFFECTS

When Oliver came to me to talk about his capacity problems, he believed his issue was time management. He had read several books and implemented multiple hacks to manage his time better, yet he still felt like his productivity needed to improve.

When I told him his problem wasn't time management or productivity but busyness, he was shocked. Most people are. It's easy to believe your busyness will decrease when your productivity increases. In part, that's true, but that's not the whole story.

Recently, I was talking with a long-time CEO of a large company. I asked him what his biggest mistake was during his time as a leader. He said, "The most unsuccessful year I ever had was the year I worked the hardest. I was doing the wrong things. I was exhausted."

This CEO demonstrates the paradox of productivity: The busier you are, the more productive you will feel, but your productivity decreases as your busyness increases.

Overcommitted people look and often feel productive, but they are not. Busyness harms your productivity.

Here are some of the effects of busyness on your productivity:

1. Busyness diminishes your excellence.

If you're like me, you don't just want to do "good enough" work. You want to be proud of the work you produce; you want excellence.

If you're overcommitted, however, you won't take the time and expend the energy to do your best work. You barely have time to deliver "good enough."

2. Busyness depletes your passion.

You got sucked into busyness by commitments that you *wanted* to make. People usually aren't overcommitted because they have to be; they're overcommitted because they said yes to too many desirable opportunities.

You want that extra project for work. You want to take that extra class to supplement your learning. You want to give your kids opportunities to play sports and learn musical instruments.

You start all those commitments with a sense of enthusiasm and passion, but when you put them all together, you quickly lose your passion—for your commitments and for life.

3. Busyness makes you feel like you've never done enough.

Back when I was suffering from busyness addiction, I frequently completed forty or more tasks in a day. I worked on multiple projects and would often switch focus dozens of times every day.

Yet, at the end of most days, I felt like I hadn't done enough. I felt like I could never do enough.

Busyness leaves you feeling like you're doing a lot but never enough. There's always one more project, twenty more tasks, more relationships you want to develop, and more commitments you want to make.

You'll feel guilty for not doing more—even though you're already doing too much.

4. Busyness exchanges accomplishment for achievement.

Busy people achieve a lot but accomplish very little. It's like running on a treadmill. You may get 15,000 steps in a run (lots of achievement), but you don't go anywhere (no accomplishment).

Achievement is doing a lot of activity, but accomplishment is when you make progress on your highest priorities.

Achievement is "busy work;" accomplishment is meaningful work.

Which do you want? Do you want to achieve or do you want to accomplish?

When you get (un)busy, you can Prioritize, Evaluate, Plan and Accomplish your highest priorities. You will still work hard, but you'll work hard to accomplish, not merely achieve.

5. Busyness sucks away your energy.

Your productivity depends on your energy. The more energy you have, the more productive you can be.

Busyness drains your energy. Rather than focusing your energy on your highest priorities, you disperse your energy in dozens of projects that makes you less productive.

Busyness convinces you that you don't have time for sleep or rest or play. All of this diminishes your energy and thus decreases your productivity.

Organizational Effects

As Oliver and I had coffee, I asked him to tell me about his company and its goals. He serves as a senior leader for a Fortune 500 company. The company has five divisions.

Two years prior, each division was responsible for identifying and executing two priorities. That's ten company priorities. Those priorities then got pushed down through the entire organization so every frontline employee had a stake in those ten priorities.

That year, the average person in his company worked forty-eight hours per week to accomplish those priorities. When I asked Oliver how the company did, he said that they had not accomplished one of those priorities, which shouldn't be shocking.

In the book *The 4 Disciplines of Execution*, the authors indicate that companies that have four or more major goals happening at one time accomplish almost none of them with excellence.[19]

I asked Oliver what the Executive Team's response to the failure was.

He responded, "The Executive Team determined that the goals must not have been inspiring enough. They assigned each division to identify *three* priorities...so fifteen goals across the organization. Now, people are working about fifty-five hours per week. People are exhausted, but the Executive Team thinks it will inspire us to have these grand goals."

I've seen the same thing multiple times in organizations from Fortune 500 companies to small churches. Leaders create a grand vision which gets people inspired. When the leaders can't figure out how to make the vision happen, they create multiple goals and often change directions every few months. Leaders think that people will be inspired to work harder and longer, but their people end up frustrated and confused. The people can't figure out how to make progress and, therefore, don't know if they're making progress.

"Oliver," I told him, "I guarantee your company won't hit any of your goals this year unless you minimize to two or three goals. Not two or three per division, just two or three goals. Your company is taking stressed, overwhelmed, and exhausted people and infecting them with more busyness. They're drowning, but instead of throwing them a life preserver, management is dumping buckets of water on their heads."

So how is busyness affecting your organization?

1. Busy organizations are full of "disengaged zombies."

If all of your employees are busy, then the workforce that's coming to their job every day is stressed, exhausted, and overwhelmed.

They're like zombies. They drag their broken-down bodies and exhausted minds to work. All their busyness is killing them. Their bodies, minds, and emotions are drained. They're also disengaged, working longer hours and taking less vacation time.

In August 2018, Gallup reported that 53% of workers are not engaged at work. "They may be generally satisfied but are not cognitively and emotionally connected to their work and workplace; they will usually show up to work and do the minimum required but will quickly leave their company for a slightly better offer."[20] Gallup recorded that the percentage of "actively disengaged" employees, those who are miserable at work and trying to sabotage the company, is at 13%.

The people who work with and for you every day are disengaged zombies. Before you get mad at them, realize that busy organizations contribute to the problem.

2. Busy organizations make busy people busier.

As I consult with companies and nonprofits, most organizations expect "more" from their people, offer little support, give few resources, and offer low pay. Like Oliver's company, they overcommit to goals and initiatives that fracture the attention of their workforce and keep them in a state of constant, frantic, and frenetic activity.

Technology has created a boundaryless office. Employees have their email with them everywhere and check their phones multiple times every night. They stay connected to work twenty-four hours a day.

As I shared earlier, the average salaried employee works forty-seven hours per week with 25% of them putting in over sixty hours.[21] They have or take fewer vacation days (only 13 days per year, down from 21 days at the turn of the century).

If employees are more connected, working longer hours, and taking less vacation, they also have less time for their other roles and responsibilities, which means that busy organizations are making busy people even busier.

Entire organizations drown in busyness as leaders absorb its effects and then leak it to all the people who work with them.

3. Busyness creates fear-based cultures.

A couple of years ago, I spent a day consulting with a nonprofit to help with strategic planning. One of the participants spoke up.

"We don't have a unifying vision. We need to be inspired to lay down our lives."

At that moment, the entire room deflated. I felt the energy in the room get sucked out. I stopped the group and asked, "Do you feel the fear?"

One of the men, Dan, dared to say, "Yes. I felt my whole body shrink."

I asked him why, and he responded, "I love this organization. I'm already laying down my life for it. Now you want a vision that's so far-reaching that I lay down *more* of my life for it. That scares me!"

Every busy person who works with you has a sympathetic nervous system that's in overdrive. They're producing massive amounts of cortisol. Remember, cortisol lowers your mood, diminishes your motivation, and raises your level of fear. *In other words, your organization is full of unhappy, unmotivated and fearful people.*

They're afraid of their boss. Afraid of what they're co-workers are thinking. Afraid to make a mistake. Afraid of layoffs. Afraid others don't like them. Afraid they won't have enough time to do everything they need to do. Afraid they're going to miss out on time with their family. Afraid they're going to get to the end of their lives, and all they'll have to show for it is that they worked for your company. Afraid you're going to ask even more of them.

Fear isn't always rational, but it is reality. Busy organizations create fear-based cultures. These work environments diminish enthusiasm and empowerment and replace it with terror.

Busyness in organizations doesn't just affect employees. It also affects customers.

4. Busy organizations generate poor customer experiences.

I recently ate at a restaurant with my dad. This restaurant usually has quality customer service, but when the waiter came to our table, she gave indications of being stressed and overwhelmed. She didn't make eye contact with us. She kept looking at her watch. She moved quickly from table to table rather than giving personalized attention. She got multiple parts of our order wrong and even delivered cold food. When I told her the food was cold, she huffed as if she was frustrated with us.

Finally, I asked her if everything was all right. She responded, "It's fine. I'm just busy." Her busyness created an unsatisfactory customer experience.

Busy people don't create great customer experiences.[22] All of the stress, overwhelm, and exhaustion will leak into their customer interactions. If you have a fear-based culture, your customers will be able to sense it. They will feel depersonalized, resented, or even actively disliked. Clients will absorb the fear and stress, and that's a recipe for terrible customer experiences.

5. Busy organizations lose value.

All of this, of course, leads to a loss of value, revenue, profit, and market share. Your company can't make the money it wants because your employees are disengaged. As a result, customers disengage as well. Nobody wants to contribute to or participate in anything that makes them feel unvalued.

I hope by now you're convinced that busyness isn't worth it. It's not worth it to sacrifice your life on the altar of overcommitment.

If that's what you've decided, then it's time for the next decision: Decide if you are too busy.

5

DECIDE IF YOU'RE TOO BUSY

I recently consulted with a group of pastors regarding busyness. They were all high functioning men and women leading growing churches. I spent part of the morning talking with them about the effects of busyness. I led them to decide if busyness was worth it for them and their congregations. All of them agreed busyness was not worth the damage it caused.

Then I asked them if they were too busy. Every single person nodded their heads in agreement—every person except Charlie.

Charlie said, "I *feel* like I'm too busy, but how do I *know* if I am?"

You may be asking the same question. There's not a magic formula for determining if you're a victim of busyness. **Busyness begins when your commitments exceed your capacity.** The amount of obligations one can handle varies from person to person, but the signs of overcommitment are the same.

SIGNS THAT YOU'RE TOO BUSY

In my years of research, I have found twenty common signs of busyness:

1. You feel exhausted when you wake up.

2. When you're working on a task, you can't focus.

3. When you get together with friends, you only have an hour.

4. You don't have any good friends with whom you regularly spend time.

5. You don't have a way of capturing all the ideas you have.

6. You don't have any hobbies or enjoyable activities that you participate in weekly.

7. When you're tired, you use caffeine to wake you up.

8. You don't take a full day off work (including work around your house) every week.

9. You don't know what your highest priorities are every week.

10. You don't take time weekly to reflect on your accomplishments from the previous week.

11. You feel exhausted when you go to bed but still feel like there's so much you didn't get done.

12. You have overlapping meetings.

13. You are late to appointments multiple times each week.

14. You check work email/voicemail after you get home.

15. You feel overwhelmed.

16. You don't have a sense of purpose to most of the activities in your life.

17. When people ask you how you're doing, you tell them you're busy.

18. You say "yes" more often than "no" when people ask you to take on a commitment.

19. You frequently wonder how you're going to "fit it all in."

20. You feel guilt or shame when you're not productive.

Want to See How Busy You Are? Take the free online assessment to evaluate your level of busyness. Go to **www. gettinunbusybook.com/assessment**.

THE BUSYNESS VORTEX

Those twenty signs listed above can help you determine if you're too busy, but there is another sign that makes it clear you're drowning in busyness. I call it the **Busyness Vortex**. **Hurry**, **Worry**, and **Scurry** create this vortex.

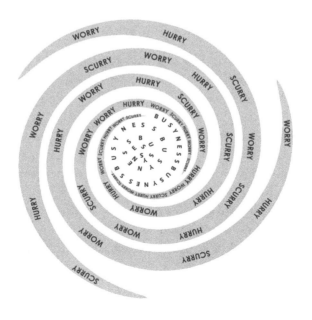

Hurry. If you're hurried, you rush from one commitment to the next. You pack your calendar with multiple appointments that overlap each other. You end one meeting at 2 pm and sprint immediately to another that starts at 2 pm.

You bolt out of your office to beat traffic. You drive fast. You hurry in the mornings to get ready because you slept through your alarm.

You scarf down your breakfast. You arrive late to appointments.

Even when you're not running late, you feel hurried. You feel like you never have enough time.

Worry. When you hurry your body, your anxiety increases. You worry you can't get all your projects finished.

You worry you're not spending enough time with your kids.

You worry you don't have enough money.

You worry you're not managing your time well, that your kids aren't doing enough to get into a good college.

You worry constantly. Fear becomes your default state of mind.

Scurry. Scurry is not a word we frequently use (unless we're talking about a mouse.) The definition of scurry is *fast and confused movement*. **Scurry** can take place in your body and mind.

Scurry occurs when you can't concentrate for long. Your mind races. It flits from one subject to another to another. It feels like you have a thousand thoughts at one time.

When you're in a meeting at work, you can't concentrate because of all the things you need to accomplish at home. At home, your mind races about work.

You can't think through your decisions but feel like you must make them quickly.

Hurry, Worry, and Scurry all flow together in your mind and body. If you Hurry with your body, it will lead you to Worry and Scurry. If you Worry with your mind, it will come out as hurriedness in your body. Any one of them—Hurry, Worry, or Scurry—could be the portal that sucks you into the Busyness Vortex. The more hurried, worried, and scurried you get, the busier you get. The busier you get, the more you experience Hurry, Worry, and Scurry.

ARE YOU TOO BUSY?

When I finished giving these examples and talking about the Busyness Vortex, I asked Charlie if he thought he was too busy.

"Absolutely," he responded.

What about you? In the last chapter, you decided if busyness was worth it. In this chapter, I encourage you to evaluate if you're too busy.

I hope you are not. I hope you're living with Purpose, Productivity, and Peace. I hope at this point, you decide you don't need this book and put it down or pass it on to someone who you think it would benefit. However, I've talked to too many people and I know that (un)busy people are not the norm.

What did you decide? Are you too busy? If so, it's time to Decide to get (un)busy.

6

DECIDE TO GET (UN)BUSY

I told you at the beginning of this section that you must make three choices: (1) Is busyness worth it? (2) Am I busy? (3) What will I do with my busyness?"

By now, I hope I've convinced you that busyness isn't worth it. It's killing you. It's not just taking away the quantity of your life, but it's diminishing the quality of your life as well.

Busyness is tricking you into believing it's good and expected of you.

If you're reading this chapter, I assume you've decided you are too busy.

Now, it's time for the third decision: What will you do with your busyness?

You have four options for responding.

FOUR POSSIBLE RESPONSES

1. Decide to Live in Resignation

You can resign yourself to the fact that you're busy, that the world is busy, and that everyone expects you to be busy. You can throw up your hands and give up. "Oh, well. I'm busy. That's life."

If that's your choice, put down the book. Don't waste any time reading something that's not going to help you.

2. Decide to Procrastinate

You could determine you're going to read the rest of this book and *then* decide what you're going to do with busyness. You may think to yourself, "I need to learn *how* to get (un)busy, and then I'll decide if I'm actually going to do it."

If that's your choice, keep reading, but remember that postponing a decision is a decision. The longer you wait to finalize a decision, the harder the choice gets.

3. Decide to Scale Back

You could decide you'll read the rest of the book and find a few new practices or hacks that can help you scale back on busyness.

This selective approach is a good option if you've got the patience. You could spend years making slow, incremental changes so that eventually, (one day in the far-distant future) you can live with Purpose, Productivity, and Peace.

If this is you, keep reading so you can discover some great hacks, but remember the power of this book is in the process, not merely in the individual tools.

4. Decide to Get (un)Busy

Your final option is to decide here and now that you're going to get (un)busy.

You know busyness is killing you. You're tired of making excuses. You're tired of believing that busyness is normal. You're tired of living a stressed, exhausted, and overwhelmed life.

You can decide to do something about it starting now. You can decide to get (un)busy.

You don't know how it's going to happen. You don't know what the rest of the process is. You may even be afraid because deciding to get (un)busy is such a life-altering decision.

Brandon Webb writes in his book *Mastering Fear: A Navy Seal's Guide*, "You might think that big decisions, potentially life-altering decisions, arise out of courage. They don't. It's the other way around. The strength and the courage to keep going arise *out of* the decision. **The decision comes first.**"[23]

FIVE ACTIONS TO DECIDE TO GET (UN)BUSY

If you're ready to get (un)busy, I want you to take five actions.

1. Write down your Gettin' (un)Busy Manifesto.

Download the Gettin' (un)Busy Manifesto template at **www.gettinunbusybook.com/tools**

Don't type it out. Write it. Studies have shown that you're 42% more likely to follow through on a commitment if you write it down.[24]

You could write something as simple as "On this day, I, [fill in your name], commit to kill busyness so it can't kill me." Perhaps "On this day, I [fill in your name] commit to get (un)busy so that I can start living with Purpose, Productivity, and Peace."

2. Sign your name to it.

You are making a contract with yourself.

3. Put the paper in prominent places.

Tape it to your computer or bathroom mirror. Take a picture of it and make it your home screen on your phone. Copy it and put it in multiple places to remind you of your commitment.

4. Say it out loud every day.

Read your commitment out loud every morning. Remind yourself of the commitment you've made. Remind yourself you want to get (un)busy so that busyness can't kill you.

5. Keep reading.

I'm so proud of you. You've just made a courageous decision to get (un)busy—even though you don't know how yet.

It's my job to help you learn how to get (un)busy. It's your job to Decide and then to follow through, so keep reading. In the next section, you'll begin to Deconstruct your beliefs, habits and (un)wanted commitments that keep you trapped in busyness.

Let me leave you with a quote from W.H. Murray, a Scottish mountain climber.

> Until one is committed, there is hesitancy, the chance to draw back, always ineffectiveness. Concerning all acts of initiative and creativity, there is one elementary truth... that the moment one definitely commits oneself, then Providence moves too. All sorts of things occur to help one that would never otherwise have occurred. A whole stream of events issues from the decision, raising in one's favor all manner of unforeseen incidents and meetings and material assistance, which no man could have dreamt would have come his way.[25]

STEP 1: GET BUSY GETTIN' (UN)BUSY

At the end of each Step, I'll include a section called "Get Busy Gettin' (un)Busy." It will recap some major insights from the Step and remind you of the actions that you need to take.

Busyness is both prevalent and expected. Because of this, Gettin' (un)Busy is unusual and unexpected! That's why the first step is to Decide. Before you can do anything about your busyness, you must make three decisions: (1) Is busyness worth it? (2) Are you busy? (3) Are you going to get (un)busy?

DECIDE IF BUSYNESS IS WORTH IT

Busyness affects you physically, mentally, emotionally, and relationally. It also affects your productivity and infects entire organizations.

- ☐ Look at the effects of busyness and decide if you think busyness is good.

- ☐ As a leader, determine if you want to build a busy organization, knowing the effects that busyness will have on its value.

DECIDE IF YOU'RE TOO BUSY

Busyness isn't just a feeling that you have. There are a lot of signs that you're too busy. The most telling is the constant Busyness Vortex of Hurry, Worry, and Scurry.

- ☐ Take the busyness assessment to see if you're too busy. Go to www.gettinunbusybook.com/assessment

- ☐ Take stock of your life to determine if you experience the Busyness Vortex.
- ☐ Decide if you're too busy and want to do something about it.

DECIDE TO GET (UN)BUSY

Gettin' (un)Busy begins with a decision about what you're going to do with your busyness. Will you resign yourself to it or procrastinate in dealing with it? Will you decide to slowly scale back or will you decide to get (un)busy?

- ☐ Write down your Gettin' (un)Busy Manifesto.
- ☐ Sign your name on it.
- ☐ Put the paper in a prominent place.
- ☐ Read it out loud every day.
- ☐ Keep reading this book.

STEP 2

DECONSTRUCT

Hoarders like Lloyd with his bicycle parts have spent years building up their storage of stuff until it overtakes their lives. Then they decide that it's time to change. That decision can be exhilarating. They may begin to see the new possibilities of life. They catch a vision for how wonderful their lives can become when they free themselves from all their stuff.

However, before they can make their vision a reality, they must go through a painful step—Deconstruction. Hoarders go through all the belongings that they've accumulated and begin to evaluate what stays and what goes. Not only do they get rid of the stuff, but they also need to get rid of old ways of thinking and behaving that got them trapped in the first place.

If you've ever watched a show about a hoarder, this process of Deconstruction can be excruciating.

Busyness is a form of hoarding. While hoarders collect tangible things, busyness addicts collect commitments, experiences, and activities. Before you can live a life of Purpose, Productivity, and Peace, you must go through this step of **Deconstruction**.

The path to peace is through Deconstruction, but it is the hardest step for overwhelmed people to accept. Most people want to jump straight from Step 1 to Step 3—from Decide to Design. They want to think about their dreams and priorities. They envision the life they want to live and long to start moving toward it.

But I have never seen that work. If you jump straight from Decide to Design, you will spend time envisioning the life you want to live. You'll create a picture of a preferred future. That picture will become a commitment, which means you'll add another commitment to an already overcommitted life. It's like telling a hoarder the best way to change their lifestyle is to envision all the stuff they're going to collect in their new house.

Deconstruction precedes Design.

You've already Decided. Now it's time to trust the process and begin Deconstruction. In this step, you'll Deconstruct:

1. **Inhibiting Beliefs.** You have ways of thinking that keep you trapped in busyness. You must address these Inhibiting Beliefs and replace them with Empowering Truths.

2. **Bad Habits.** Busyness comes from a few bad habits that you unknowingly developed. You'll need to change these habits to move forward.

3. **(un)Wanted Commitments.** To free yourself from too many obligations, get (un)committed. You must inventory and diminish your responsibilities.

7

DECONSTRUCT INHIBITING BELIEFS

Don was a successful (and busy) attorney. He was gone multiple nights each week from his family. He loved his wife and kids, and he felt guilty he was gone so much. He and his wife barely spoke. He rarely saw his kids. He wanted to be a better dad and husband, but he also wanted to be a great attorney.

One weekend, he rented a boat and took his wife and kids out on a lake. At the end of the day, they all felt closer to each other. They had fun together and felt like a family for the first time in years. A few weeks later, Don rented a boat again and got the same results. The dynamics in his family improved.

That's when he made a decision that changed everything. He decided to buy a boat. He reasoned the family could go on the lake any time they wanted to spend time together.

To buy the boat, though, Don needed more money. He secured a few more clients and worked extra nights. His family understood the reason, though, so they didn't mind and supported him for the end goal. For the next few months, he found new clients and worked late hours to help them. When he was home, he researched boats.

After several months, Don bought the new boat. The family got up early one Saturday morning, loaded into the truck and drove to the lake. It took a while to get the boat in the water. When they had rented boats, they hadn't needed to worry about this. But, by the time they left the lake, they had enjoyed another great day. It was even better because it was *their* boat.

After he got home, Don needed to clean the boat. He realized he didn't have all the necessary supplies, so he had to drive to the store. He spent the evening scrubbing the boat, but he couldn't get it all finished.

He got up early on Sunday and spent most of the morning finishing cleaning the boat. He convinced himself it was taking so long because of the learning curve, and the process would eventually be easier and quicker. The next week, he had to work several nights at the office to keep up with the client load he had generated to buy the boat.

For the first few months, the family spent many weekends on the boat. Time on the boat was delightful. However, Don dreaded not only having to clean it but also make small repairs to it. He found upgrades that he wanted, which required extra money. After a few months, Don found himself spending more time with the boat than with his family.

Don bought the boat because he wanted to spend more time with his most cherished people, but the reality was Don spent more time away from his family so that he could spend more time with them. The math didn't work.

A year after he bought the boat, the family only went to the lake about once every other month. After two years, the boat sat covered and unused most of the time. They finally sold it. He went back to his old way of working, and the family once again grew distant.

Don's busyness existed before he bought the boat, and it continued after he sold the boat. Don desired to be a better dad and husband, but he thought the remedy was adding *more* commitments.

Busyness is all about adding *more*. After spending years with busy people, I've discovered three **Inhibiting Beliefs** that keep you trapped in busyness:

(1) Identity—I need to **be** more.
(2) Activity—I need to **do** more.
(3) Quantity—I need to **get** more.

Don wanted to **be** more for his wife and kids. He wanted to **do** more with them. To do that, he believed he needed to **get** more by purchasing a boat.

What if the solution to getting more is not addition, but subtraction? Before adding anything else to his life, Don first needed to subtract Inhibiting Beliefs that kept him trapped in busyness.

You, too, must Deconstruct these three Inhibiting Beliefs and replace them with Empowering Truths.

IDENTITY – I NEED TO BE MORE

When I started researching busyness, I thought of it as merely a time management issue. I believed that if I could learn to handle my calendar and project management tools better, I could get (un)busy. I had already read hundreds of books and articles on time management and implemented many of the best practices, yet I was still busy. I had to deal with the unwanted reality that busyness was not a calendar issue. There was something more consequential buried underneath my rubble of appointments.

A quote from Tim Kreider helped me see how deep the issue of busyness is. He writes, "Busyness serves as a kind of existential reassurance, a hedge against emptiness. Obviously, your life cannot possibly be silly or trivial or meaningless if you are so busy, completely booked, in demand every hour of the day."[26]

Busyness, I discovered, is not simply a calendar issue. *It is an identity issue.* It stems from a misperception of your *self*—who you really are.

The writings of Brené Brown helped me discover what the identity issue was. Brown, a shame researcher, helped me see that busyness emerges from shame. She defines shame as "the intensely painful feeling or experience of believing that we are flawed and therefore unworthy of love and belonging."[27]

How does busyness emerge from shame? The answer to this question is not easy. I spent years trying to understand and articulate the link between busyness and shame. I eventually discovered a sequence of five **Mental Moves** that connects shame and busyness. These five Mental Moves happen subconsciously and within a fraction of a second, which is why they've been so difficult to pinpoint.

What are the Mental Moves that cause busyness to emerge from shame?

Mental Move #1: You desire to be better.

In this first move, you desire to be better at something. You want to be a better employee or public speaker or mother. You want to get in better physical shape.

When you desire to be better, you create a picture in your mind of a better *future you*.

There is nothing wrong with this desire to be better. It's a trait that separates humans from animals. Humans can see ourselves as being better than we currently are and work to make that improvement happen. These abilities lead to the next Mental Move, which is where our Inhibiting Beliefs begin.

Mental Move #2: You see your *present self* as fundamentally flawed.

As you envision the *future you*, your *present you* sees yourself as flawed. It's more than the accurate perception of having room for improvement. You tend to look at your *present you* through a much more critical lens. You see yourself—at the core of your being—as fundamentally flawed.

It's not simply that you would benefit from upgrades. You see yourself as broken and inadequate.

Mental Move #3: You convince yourself that you are unworthy and not enough.

As soon as you see your *present self* as flawed, shame kicks in. Remember Brown's definition of shame: "the intensely painful feeling or experience of believing that we are *flawed* and therefore *unworthy* of love and belonging."

When you see yourself as fundamentally flawed, you convince yourself that you are not worthy. You convince yourself that you are not enough.

Your desire for improvement has become an identity issue.

Mental Move #4: You ask yourself, "What can I *do* to make myself *enough*?"

When you believe you are not enough, your subconscious umps into action to figure out what would make you enough.

You begin thinking about what you need to *do* to make yourself worthy. Notice the word "do." If you are not *enough*, it's easy to believe that you need to add something to make yourself enough.

Busyness emerges from your search for what more you can do.

Mental Move #5: You add commitments to make yourself *enough*.

You begin adding commitments (the next Inhibiting Belief) to make yourself enough. You decide to work out more. You give more time to community service. You read more books. You buy a boat. Shame drives you to more commitments, and added commitments lead you to busyness.

In an ironic twist, you become busy to compensate for shame, but your busyness will not lead you to fulfill your desire to be better.

The opposite will happen. The busier you are, the less likely you are to live up to your *future self.* Your desire to be better will once again emerge, throwing you right back into this sequence. Your shame will increase as will your busyness.

Let's apply this sequence of five Mental Moves to Don's life.

Mental Move #1: Don desired to be a better husband and father.

Don envisioned a *future Don* that was engaged in his family's life, which is what instigated him renting the boat. After a weekend of laughing and enjoying his wife and kids, he saw a *future Don* that had a thriving relationship with his family.

Healthy involvement with his loved ones was a good desire.

Mental Move #2: He saw *present Don* as fundamentally flawed.

Don's vision of being a better husband and dad led him to see *present Don* as flawed. Rather than seeing himself as a husband and father who loved his family but had room for improvement, Don only saw what was lacking. He believed, at the core of his being, that he was a bad husband and father.

Mental Move #3: Don convinced himself that he was unworthy and not enough.

When Don saw himself as fundamentally flawed, shame emerged. He believed his flaws made him unworthy and not enough. He believed his issue was not about upgrading his competency; it was overhauling his character.

Mental Move #4: Don asked himself, "What can I *do* to make myself *enough*?"

At first, Don answered that question by renting a boat and spending quality time with his family. When that went well, Don determined that he could be enough by spending more time on the boat. Therefore, to make himself *enough*, Don decided he would buy a boat.

Mental Move #5: Don added commitments to make himself *enough*.

The Inhibiting Belief of identity drove Don to do more (work longer hours, spend more time with the family, take care of the boat). It also fueled him to get more (more money, buying a boat, more time and experiences with the family).

ACTIVITY – I NEED TO DO MORE

When Don determined he needed to be a better husband and father, he didn't decide to do *less*. He didn't take on fewer clients. He didn't come home earlier to have dinner with the kids. Don took on *more*. He worked longer so he could buy a boat. He spent time on the boat. He tried to become a better husband and father by stuffing more activity into an overcommitted life.

Once shame convinces you that you need to be more, the automatic response is to act. You convince yourself, "If I need to *be* more, then I need to *do* more." Read more books. Accomplish more tasks. Take on more projects. Post more on social media.

This year, my family moved into a new house. We've been working a lot of evenings and weekends trying to get settled. Yesterday, we spent four hours on house projects—after I had worked a full day. I got in bed tired. But I found myself feeling shame about all the things that we haven't accomplished yet.

I started thinking, "I need to be a better homeowner." Within a few minutes, I had nearly convinced myself that I had enough energy to work another hour, maybe two. Fortunately, before I brewed coffee and got back to work, I caught the Inhibiting Beliefs.

Shame not only convinces you that you need to *be* more, it convinces you that you need to *do* more. When you do more, it feels good. At least in the beginning. Shame leads to stress which leads to the release of adrenaline. Adrenaline feels good. When you accomplish something, dopamine (one of the chemicals responsible for feeling happy) gets released into your body, which feels good.

All of these good feelings, though, eventually trap you in busyness by, once again, convincing you that you need to be more. Chuck DeGroat writes:

> "With a few small successes, we feel a surge of dopamine glory that fuels our addictive patterns of busyness, a sense that we've conquered the supposed enemy within. We ride this new wave as long as we can. Maybe it lasts hours, maybe even days. But sooner or later, the annoying ache is triggered again, perhaps by a deadline reminder or a critical email or a silence that lasts a bit too long. This time, it's the inner voice that doubles down. *Instead of saying I'm not doing enough, the stranger within offers a more troubling observation, I'm not enough.*"[28]

QUANTITY – I NEED TO GET MORE

The shame of feeling like you need to *be* more also leads to another Inhibiting Belief: you need to *get* more.

Shame often convinces you that you don't have enough. You need more. This need for more has two different expressions: the **economic** expression says, "I need to get more *stuff.*" The **experiential** expression says, "I need to have more *experiences.*"

Don's story demonstrates both perceived needs for getting more. When he convinced himself that he wanted to be more as a husband and father, he discovered that boating helped him do that. This solution led to a belief that he needed to get more *stuff* (a boat, a trailer, upgrades to make the boat better), and he needed to have more *experiences* (time on the lake with the family).

THE ECONOMIC MORE

In the economic version of "I need more," you believe that you need more stuff. You need a boat. You need a new book. You need a bigger house. You need face moisturizer.

I don't want to mislead you into believing that you don't have any needs. We all have some necessities—just not as many as we convince ourselves we need. That's why I don't call the Economic More a lie. It's an Inhibiting Belief.

You may need more. You may need a bigger house because you just had triplets. You may need that new book because you're learning how to market your new business. You may need face moisturizer because your skin is dry.

The problem is that the more stuff you get, the more you have to do. Randy Frazee points out, "...with increased resources comes increased complexity, not simplicity. If they aren't especially careful, the ones who have more actually have more with which to destroy themselves."[29]

When Don rented a boat, his family had a great time on the lake. When Don bought the boat, he spent more time cleaning and repairing it. Owning the boat eventually owned Don.

THE EXPERIENTIAL MORE

We don't simply want more stuff; we want more meaning in our lives. According to Gary Cross, "Busyness is more; it is the opportunity to intensify sense experience.... *(Busyness) is the promise of more life per life.*"[30]

While the Economic More focuses on the quantity of things you have, the Experiential More concentrates on the quality of your experiences. It's the belief that you need more and better experiences to improve the quality of your life.

From elaborate vacations to self-help books, to career-path opportunities and gourmet restaurants, people today have more options for a more meaningful life than ever before. Wanting a more meaningful life is not wrong. It's probably one of the reasons you're reading this book. You want to get (un)busy because you want more out of life than it's giving you. That's not a misguided desire.

I want more out of my life, and I want you to have more out of your life. However, the path to getting more out of life is not to cram more experiences into life. *The path to more is less.*

Less doesn't only mean less stuff. Minimizing is a trendy topic right now. Enter any bookstore and you will have no problem finding a book on tidying up, decluttering, or downsizing your home. Many of these books conclude that by reducing all the stuff in your life, you will have more time and money left for experiences.

There is a problem with this thinking, though. The root issues that drove you to acquire too much stuff in the first place remain unaddressed. Minimizing identifies the problems of the Economic More and provides a solution. But it ignores the problems that come with the Experiential More. You may tidy up your house, but your underlying, Inhibiting Beliefs are left undisturbed. The only thing that has changed is the way that you express your need for more.

REPLACE INHIBITING BELIEFS WITH EMPOWERING TRUTHS

There may be other Inhibiting Beliefs that keep you trapped in busyness, but I've found these three to be the most pervasive. Now that you know these three Inhibiting Beliefs, you'll become aware of how much they drive your incessant activity. You'll notice how often you convince yourself that you need to be more, do more or get more.

If you try to get (un)busy before addressing your Inhibiting Beliefs, you will quickly slip back into overcommitment—just like Don. The sad reality of his life is that Inhibiting Beliefs sabotaged his aspiration to be a better husband and father and kept him trapped in busyness. In the end, buying a boat caused Don to become even more disengaged.

Now that you've identified the Inhibiting Beliefs that drive busyness, replace them with **Empowering Truths.**

How do you replace Inhibiting Beliefs with Empowering Truths? There are four steps:

1. Record your Inhibiting Beliefs. If you can't name your Inhibiting Beliefs, you can't replace them. Write down the perceptions you have that keep you trapped in busyness. When you feel stressed, exhausted, and overwhelmed from busyness, it's coming from an Inhibiting Belief. Write it down.

2. Review your Inhibiting Beliefs. Look at what you've written down. Review it to ask yourself the question, "Do I truly believe this?" There is a difference between *feeling* that something is true in the moment and *believing* that something is true in reality. Do you *really* believe that you need to be more, do more, and get more?

3. Reject your Inhibiting Beliefs. Once you know you don't truly believe that Inhibiting Belief, reject it. This purging is both a one-time act and an ongoing decision. You reject it now and you'll need to reject it again when it rears its ugly head.

4. Replace your Inhibiting Beliefs with Empowering Truths. To get rid of your Inhibiting Beliefs, replace them with Empowering Truths. Here are some examples that helped me deal with each of the Inhibiting Beliefs.

- I replaced "I need to be more" with "my identity is rooted in who I am not what I achieve."

- I replaced "I need to do more" with "my significance is not found in the fullness of my calendar."
- I replaced "I need to get more" with "I have everything I need and more stuff only makes me busier."

Here are some Empowering Truths that you may want to consider:

- I need relationships not more possessions.
- The quality of my life will be measured by the depth of my friendships not the size of my bank account.
- The quality of my experiences is determined by the people I'm with not by the places I go.
- There is always more to do, but I don't necessarily need to do more.
- The secret to accomplishment and fulfillment is to do less not more.
- Overcommitment diminishes significance.
- When I feel overwhelmed, I need to do less not more.
- I need to commit to less to have more time, energy, attention, and impact.
- My identity is not rooted in my achievements or accomplishments.
- I am loved by others even if I don't accomplish anything.
- I am worthy of love and belonging. My achievements don't make me more or less deserving of them.

- Busyness will only make me feel better for a little while. After that, I'll feel more stressed, exhausted, and overwhelmed.

- I can do anything I want, but I can't do everything at once.

Now it's your turn. Download the Empowering Truths Worksheet from **www.gettinunbusybook.com/tools**. Record your Inhibiting Beliefs. Review, reject, and then replace them.

You're on your way to deconstructing busyness in your life. Now that you've deconstructed Inhibiting Beliefs, it's time to Deconstruct Bad Habits.

8

DECONSTRUCT BAD HABITS

You weren't born busy. Nobody is. You may have been born into a busy family. You may have learned busyness from them, but you weren't born busy.

Busyness started at a specific moment in your life when your commitments exceeded your capacity. Take a moment to think about when that moment may have been for you. My moment occurred during my junior year of college.

That semester is the first time that I remember feeling overextended. My responsibilities exceeded my time and energy capacities. But I failed to change course. Instead, I buckled into busyness, shifted into high gear, and didn't look back until it almost killed me.

You weren't born busy. You became busy. Busyness, you see, is a habit. William James wrote, "All our life, so far as it has definite form, is but a mass of habits."

Maybe that's not entirely accurate. Busyness is the mass that evolves from a *few* Bad Habits. If you can identify those habits and address them, you can begin to Deconstruct busyness.

Busyness forms from at least two unintentional habits. When you can replace those Bad Habits with good ones, deconstruction begins.

Bad Habit #1: Saying yes too quickly and too often.

Good Habit #1: Default to *no*; defend to *yes*.
Bad Habit #2: Living without boundaries.
Good Habit #2: Building and protecting strong boundaries.

Here's how you can replace those Bad Habits with good ones that will help you get (un)busy.

GOOD HABIT #1: DEFAULT TO NO; DEFEND TO YES

You have in your arsenal one of the most powerful weapons to fight and destroy busyness. You've known this weapon and yielded it well from the time that you could talk.

You could use this weapon when you were a small child. It is the favorite word of many one-year-olds.

It's the word *no*. Warren Buffet said, "The difference between successful people and really successful people is that really successful people say no to almost everything."

Busy people have a difficult time saying no. **They default to *yes* and defend their *no*.**

Whenever you ask a busy person to take on an extra commitment and add something to their plate, their default response will be *yes*. When someone asks them to do something, it's as if they believe they must do it because they are morally obligated. **They default to *yes*.**

If for some reason, they cannot do it, they will say no, but they won't just say no and move on. They will give reasons why they can't do it. **They defend their *no*.** Defending *no* opens the door for the person who's asking to challenge their reasons or to solve the problems that their reasons impose.

- If you can't do it because the time doesn't work out, then let's find another time to do it.

- If you're overcommitted, then don't worry, it will only take a little time each week.

I got sucked into busyness during my junior year by defaulting to *yes* and defending my *no*. Before the school year started, I had a full course load, a new job, and an on-campus leadership position. I was also training for my first mountain bike race.

That's when Amy, a friend of mine, invited me to interview for another volunteer organization. I should have thanked her and simply said "no." Instead, I offered a reason.

I said, "I don't think the role suits me."

My excuse gave her the opportunity to counter with, "You'll never know until you try."

I came up with another reason. "I have a lot to do this semester."

She had an answer for that, too. "This position won't require that much time, just one or two hours every week."

"I don't think I have the skills you're looking for," I argued.

"Just come to the interview, and let us determine if you have the skills."

I relented and signed up for an interview. Afterward, the team invited me to join the organization.

My mind responded, *I'm not interested.* But my mouth said, "I don't think I have the time."

"Just try it out and see if you can find the time," she said.

I had run out of arguments.

That's the moment that I became busy. I defaulted to *yes*. I defended my *no*. As a result, Amy easily overcame my *no*.

If you're going to get (un)busy, you must change this habit. Learn to **Default to *no* and Defend your *yes*.**

First, make *no* your default answer. Rather than having *yes* as your automatic response, make it *no*. When someone asks you to commit to something else, your first inclination should be *no*.

Don't just change your default, though. Change the way you say *no*. Make *no* a complete sentence.

When you say *no*, you don't need to explain it, defend it, or give a rationale for it. You don't need to apologize for it. Just say, "No, I can't do that." Or, if you're from the South like me, "thank you, but *no*." (We feel compelled to interact with people like we take our tea—never without a little sugar.)

Over my years of coaching people, I've seen people squirm when they think about saying *no*. They're afraid that they'll offend people or lose friendships. Rest assured, I've never seen anyone lose a friend when they said *no*.

It really is as simple as the old anti-drug campaign slogan: "Just say *no*." *No* is a muscle. The more you exercise it, the easier it becomes to use. You can strengthen it just like any other muscle. It may be flimsy right now, but your *no* will get stronger. It can get so strong that you will rarely need to say it because people won't ask you to make a commitment unless they are confident that you will say *yes*.

Build a new habit of defaulting to *no*, but don't stop there. Default to *no* and Defend your *yes*.

What does it mean to **Defend your *yes***? A well-defended *yes* has three characteristics:

1. A well-defended *yes* is slow. Slow down before you say *yes*. Don't rush into making a commitment. Take time before you say *yes*. You can say, "I'm interested in this. I need 24 hours to think about it." Make your *no* fast and your *yes* slow.

2. A well-defended *yes* is careful. Think through the decision before you say *yes*. If you add a new commitment, consider the ramifications it will have. Do you already have obligations that conflict with this new responsibility? Will this undertaking add value to your life and others, and are you the best person for

it? Do you know someone else who would be better? Does this opportunity advance your biggest dreams and highest priorities?

3. A well-defended *yes* subtracts. Don't just add commitments; subtract them. Your time, energy, and attention are limited. If you decide to add something new to your life, remove other responsibilities. *It takes both addition and subtraction to multiply your accomplishments.*

The first bad habit you must **Deconstruct** is your habit of saying *yes* too quickly. Replace that bad habit with a new habit: Default to *no*; Defend your *yes*. Now for the second habit.

Good Habit #2: Build Your Boundaries

Imagine that you are in the stands at a football game. The quarterback takes the snap. You notice one of the wide receivers run five yards down and then turn right. He runs past the sidelines and into the stands. He disappears into the tunnel, only to emerge on the second level. The receiver then throws his hands up in the air and screams, "I'm open! I'm open!"

You would think, *that wide receiver is crazy*. He may be open, but he's not in the field of play. He is out of bounds. Even if he catches the ball, the play doesn't count.

Boundaries give guidance to games. Without sidelines, football would be confusing and chaotic. In the same way, life without boundaries leads to chaos:

- You work until you're exhausted and collapse into bed.

- You take on more commitments than you can complete.

- You act as if you have unlimited time, energy, and attention.

One of the worst habits of busy people is the refusal to accept their limitations. To deconstruct this bad habit, build three types of boundaries in your life.

1. End-of-Day Boundaries

The End-of-Day Boundary is a line that you draw on your calendar that says, *at this time, all work stops.* Not just your job, but all work. House projects. Homework. Checking email.

When my family started Gettin' (un)Busy, we identified 9:00 pm as our End-of-Day Boundary. If the kitchen still needed to be cleaned, it would have to wait until the next day. If the kids hadn't completed homework by that time, they weren't going to get it finished.

You may be thinking, "But how will we get it all done?" The End-of-Day Boundary (like the other boundaries) hinges on Parkinson's Law: "work expands to fill the time allotted."[31] In other words, if you allow three hours to work on a project, it will take three hours. But if you only give the project two hours, you'll probably complete it in that time.

Without boundaries, you allot infinite time for all your responsibilities. When you build an End-of-Day Boundary, you limit the amount of time you work. By adding restrictions, you'll discover that you accomplish more in less time.

You'll also realize that, when you don't complete the work by the end of day, it's not the end of the world.

2. Work Day Boundaries.

The second kind of boundary focuses on when your *job* ends every day. When I was working with Oliver, I asked when he would go home at night. "It depends on what I'm working on." Sometimes it's 6:00, but usually an hour or two later."

I asked him, "When you get home, do you do any work?"

He admitted he usually checked and responded to his email.

I encouraged him to build a work day boundary—to pick a time at which his job finished each day. No more work. No more email.

He picked 6:00 pm. He set an alarm for 5:45 pm to let him know he needed to walk out the door in fifteen minutes.

It took him a couple of weeks to get used to the idea of being finished by that time, but he found he was getting the same amount of work finished as before. Why? Because "work expands to fill the time allotted." If you shrink the allocated time, you can usually get as much finished.

3. Task Boundaries.

There are some tasks you hate to do. They suck the life out of you. It could be filling out your expense reports at work or cleaning your bathroom at home.

When you have a job that you hate, it often takes longer to accomplish because it drains your energy. Task Boundaries can help you complete these disliked responsibilities quickly.

Here's how: Give yourself a realistic but challenging amount of time to complete a job. You may even want to write it in your calendar and schedule something before and after to strengthen your boundaries.

Dorothy and I hate grocery shopping. Each time we pass through those automatic sliding doors, we feel as if we are characters in a sci-fi movie, trapped on a planet where time passes more quickly than on Earth. Before we know it, we are caught in a black hole of unexpected specials, nutrition label comparisons, and new product evaluations. The sun was up when we entered, but we are shocked when we step out into darkness, asking one another, "How long were we in there?"

Our best solution has been to set up a Task Boundary. Now, when we drop off a kid for an hour-long activity, we hit the grocery store. We know that we have less than sixty minutes to be back for pick-up, and we cannot allow ourselves to get sucked into the time warp.

By restricting the amount of time you allocate for a task, you'll get it done more quickly.

As I've said, the first time I remember feeling trapped in overcommitment was my junior year of college. In order to keep up with all my responsibilities, I kept pushing myself toward Bad Habits. Have you identified when your Bad Habits began? Busy people have developed Bad Habits, and you must deconstruct those habits if you're going to get (un)busy.

Once you Deconstruct Bad Habits, replace them with good ones:

Bad Habit #1: Saying yes too quickly and too often.
Good Habit #1: Default to *no*; defend to *yes*.
Bad Habit #2: Living without boundaries.
Good Habit #2: Building and protecting strong boundaries.

Now it's time for the last objective in this step – Deconstruct (un)Wanted Commitments.

9

DECONSTRUCT (UN)WANTED COMMITMENTS

A couple of years after Dr. Tate told me that busyness was killing me, I woke up with heart palpitations on Saturday morning. I had been making slow progress on the process of gettin' (un)busy, but I was still trapped. Unsure what was causing the palpitations, I decided to journal through my obligations to discover where I felt higher stress levels.

Several responsibilities were causing stress, but when I wrote the words *Project Management Launch*, my heart raced like a Kentucky Derby horse.

A few months prior, I had taken on a new project at work. A senior leader assembled a cross-functional team to determine and rollout an organization-wide project management system.

I saw it as a great career opportunity that could benefit the whole organization and align with my passion for project management. But I had hesitated when the leader invited me to join the team. Not only was I still overcommitted, but I was also beginning the dissertation phase of my doctoral work, which would require significant amounts of reading and writing.

I expressed my concern to the leader. He assured me the work project would have a six-month deadline, so I accepted the opportunity with enthusiasm.

As is the case with most projects, the scope and complexity quickly expanded. The team grew to eleven people, which increased the number of communication channels and the difficulty in scheduling team meetings. The project timeline grew from six months to eighteen. Worse, the team leader was a man of shady integrity and self-interest. It became clear that his reason for leading the team wasn't to help the organization but to advance his standing in the company.

Since the team had several dispersed offices, I had to travel multiple times each month through Atlanta. Atlanta's terrible traffic meant early mornings and late nights to participate in meetings that only lasted a few hours. There were also major leadership changes happening, so the team was uncertain whether this project management solution would stick.

After two months on the team, I found myself dreading everything about it. Every interaction about the project (there were multiple every day) caused my adrenaline and cortisol levels to skyrocket.

Dr. Tate had warned me that I needed to kill busyness before it killed me, but I had just inflicted another wound on myself by joining the team.

Once I identified the Project Management Launch as the primary culprit of my heart palpitations, I brainstormed my options. I had three:

1. Stick with the team for eighteen months, giving up family and personal time and staying trapped in busyness.

2. Give a half-hearted effort to the team and live with the shame that I didn't give it my all.

3. Deconstruct my commitment to the team.

I chose to deconstruct this (un)wanted commitment. *I committed to (un)commit.* I pulled out of the project, explaining

I was overcommitted. I offered to stay on the team for one more month while I found a suitable replacement. As soon as I stepped down, I felt the stress, overwhelm, and exhaustion diminish.

If you're going to get (un)busy, you must Deconstruct Inhibiting Beliefs and Bad Habits. You also need to Deconstruct (un)Wanted Commitments. You must commit to (un)commit.

COMMIT TO (UN)COMMIT

There are a million reasons you overcommit.

- You're a people pleaser who can't say no.

- You get excited by new opportunities and possibilities.

- You get bored by the same routines and want to do something new.

- You feel obligated to help people and say yes to avoid feeling guilty.

- You love to help other people because it makes you feel good about yourself.

Whatever the reason(s), you're busy because you commit.
And commit.
And commit.
And commit.

Here you are now, ready to get (un)busy. You want to live with Purpose, Productivity, and Peace. You've already deconstructed some of your beliefs and habits. Now it's time to Deconstruct some of your commitments.

It's time to commit to (un)commit.

It won't be easy, but it's worth it. By the end of this chapter, you will have a list of commitments that you will (un)commit from and a plan of how you're going to (un)commit. By the time you finish the plan, you will have freed up ten or more hours every week in your life.

STEPS TO COMMIT TO (UN)COMMIT

Commit to (un)commit in six actions. You can do this exercise on a sheet of paper or download the Commit to (un)Commit Worksheet from **www.gettinunbusybook.com/tools**. Start by making five columns.

Commitment	Time	Feeling	Action	Step

1. Identify all your commitments.

In the first step, identify all the commitments that take up your time. On the piece of paper, make five columns that look like this.

Commitment	Time	Feeling	Action	Step
Meal preparation				
Take kids to and from school				
Board meeting				
Expense reports				

Start writing down all your commitments. Be specific. Don't merely say your time goes to your job. What are all the commitments you have within your job? Think about daily, weekly, and monthly commitments you make.

- Meetings
- Reports
- Individuals you supervise
- Projects
- Family commitments
- Activities you attend (or for which you provide transportation)
- Meals you prepare
- Chores you perform
- Community service
- Travel
- Exercise

Identify all the commitments you have.

You may need to pull out your calendar and look over the last three months. You probably have a lot of small commitments that occur infrequently but require time, energy, and attention.

Once you've written all your commitments down, stop and review your list.\. Many of the people I've worked with are astounded by how extensive it is.

2. Write down how long each commitment takes.

You don't need to be precise. Just estimate.

Commitment	Time	Feeling	Action	Step
Meal preparation	1 hour per day			
Take kids to and from school	45 minutes per day			
Board meeting	8 hours per quarter			
Expense reports	30 minutes per month			

3. Identify your feelings about each commitment.

In the third column, identify how you feel about each commitment. Don't worry; you're not going to categorize complex emotions about each responsibility. Just use three emojis to identify how you feel.

☺ **Yeah!** You love this commitment. It brings you a sense of joy and purpose. You get excited before you do this and feel energized after you do it. You often feel like you're making a contribution to others when you do this.

☹ **Nah!** Even though it's a "good commitment," you don't enjoy it. You dread it before you do it and feel drained of energy afterward. You wish you didn't have to fulfill this obligation. Even if other people benefit from your contribution, it doesn't feel like a significant impact.

😐 **Meh!** You don't feel anything about this responsibility. You're ambivalent to it, feeling neither excitement nor dread. It's neutral.

Commitment	Time	Feeling	Action	Step
Meal preparation	1 hour per day	😃		
Take kids to and from school	45 minutes per day	😐		
Board meeting	8 hours per quarter	😃		
Expense reports	30 minutes per month	😐		

Here are a couple of tips that can help you discover your feeling toward each commitment.

- Don't think about each one for more than three seconds. Go with your initial reaction.

- If you are stuck or aren't sure how you feel, give it a "meh."

- You often find that your deepest sense of energy and enjoyment results in your greatest impact on others. Keep that in mind for the next step.

4. Determine your (un)commitment action.

Go through each of your "meh" and "nah" reactions. To the best of your ability, commit to (un)commit from these responsibilities because they diminish your time, energy, attention, and impact. To help you get free from these duties, you have four possible actions:

1. *Quit.* If it doesn't need to be done, stop. Stop showing up. Stop attending the Book Club if you're not

getting anything from it. Don't sign up for the Lunch and Learn if you're not expected to go.

2. *Delegate.* If the responsibility needs to be done, *you* don't have to be the person who does it. Delegate (un) Wanted Commitments. Hire a part-time assistant to do your expense reports and calendaring. Hire a maid service to clean your house, or give your children more household responsibilities.

3. *Negotiate.* If the commitment needs to be done but you don't love it, see if you can exchange services with someone else. Negotiate a carpool system with a neighbor.

I did this with a co-worker recently. I love to create content but hate to design materials for the content I produce. One of my co-workers dreads content creation but loves designing. We worked out a deal where I help her with content design, and she helps me with material design.

Before I tell you the fourth option, there's one important note. Whether you quit, delegate or negotiate, you want to do this with honor. Don't break promises that you've made. If you promised to help with a service opportunity for a year, keep your word, but dedicate that you will (un)commit from the service opportunity when the year is done.

4. *Accept it.* If you don't have any way of getting out of the obligation, then keep it. But don't simply keep it. Accept it. We all have responsibilities that we don't love. Aim to have as few of them as possible. If you must keep a task, then don't resent it. Accept it as part of life.

Commitment	Time	Feeling	Action	Step
Meal preparation	1 hour per day	☺		
Take kids to and from school	45 minutes per day	☺	Negotiate	
Board meeting	8 hours per quarter	☺		
Expense reports	30 minutes per month	☺	Delegate	

5. Choose your next action.

For each (un)commitment you're making, determine your next action. You must do something.

- If you're quitting your book club, tell the leader you'll no longer be there.

- If you're delegating a report to your administrative assistant, document the process and schedule time to train him or her on how to prepare the report.

- If you're negotiating getting kids to school, talk to your neighbor about carpooling.

Determine the next step to take for every action you quit, delegate or negotiate.

Commitment	Time	Feeling	Action	Step
Meal preparation	1 hour per day	😊		
Take kids to and from school	45 minutes per day	😐	Negotiate	Talk to Brandy about carpool options.
Board meeting	8 hours per quarter	😊		
Expense reports	30 minutes per month	🙁	Delegate	Research an hourly virtual assistant.

6. Do It!

Congratulations, you've done the most difficult part! You've determined the obligations that you no longer want. You've decided whether you're going to quit, delegate, negotiate, or keep each of those commitments. And you've chosen the next action.

Now act. Do what you've pledged to do. It's going to take some time to quit, delegate, or negotiate, but, by the end, you will have deconstructed a significant amount of your busyness. Many people get back at least ten hours every week.

Busyness is full of good responsibilities that leave you overcommitted. If you're going to get (un)busy, you must commit to (un)commit.

Now you're ready for the next step, Design.

STEP 2: GET BUSY GETTIN' (UN)BUSY

Busyness is a form of hoarding. While hoarders collect stuff, busyness addicts collect commitments, experiences, and activities. Before you can live a life of Purpose, Productivity, and Peace, you must go through this step of Deconstructing Inhibiting Beliefs, Bad Habits, and (un)Wanted Commitments.

DECONSTRUCT INHIBITING BELIEFS

Three Inhibiting Beliefs keep you trapped in busyness: (1) Identity: I need to be more; (2) Activity: I need to do more; and (3) Quantity: I need to get more. If you're going to get (un)busy, replace these Inhibiting Beliefs with Empowering Truths.

- ☐ Record your Inhibiting Beliefs.
- ☐ Review your Inhibiting Beliefs to ask if you believe they are true.
- ☐ Reject your Inhibiting Beliefs that you don't believe.
- ☐ Replace your Inhibiting Beliefs with Empowering Truths.

DECONSTRUCT BAD HABITS

Busyness began at a specific moment in your life when your commitments exceeded your capacity. To keep up with your responsibilities, you've developed Bad Habits that keep you trapped in busyness. You must Deconstruct those Bad Habits and replace them with two good habits: (1) Default to *no* and Defend to *yes* and (2) Build your Boundaries.

- ☐ Make *no* your default answer when someone (including yourself) asks you to take on a new project.

- ☐ Defend your *yes* by slowing down and thinking through your decisions before you add another obligation.

- ☐ Establish your End-of-Day Boundary at which point all household work stops.

- ☐ Determine your Workday Boundaries.

- ☐ Develop Task Boundaries around jobs that you hate to do so that you can accomplish them quickly.

DECONSTRUCT (UN)WANTED COMMITMENTS

You're busy because you're overcommitted. To deconstruct busyness, you must commit to (un)commit.

- ☐ Identify all your commitments.

- ☐ Write down how long each one takes.

- ☐ Identify your feelings about each one.

- ☐ Go through all "meh" and "nah" responsibilities to decide if you will quit, delegate, negotiate, or accept each one.

- ☐ Choose your next step for each commitment from which you're (un)committing.

- ☐ Do the next steps that you selected.

STEP 3

DESIGN

Now that you've Deconstructed Inhibiting Beliefs, Bad Habits, and (un)Wanted Commitments, it's time to begin the third step—**Design**. In this step, you envision the life that you want to live. But there is a common mistake you could make that this point. You could start with identifying and planning out your dreams and goals. I promise you that you'll do that by the end of this section, but if you jump straight to that action, you're likely to go right back to busyness.

Dreams and goals will fuel you, but they can also consume and eventually exhaust you. Before we get to your dreams and priorities, you will Design two elements.

First, you'll Design the **Pace and Space** of life you want. Pace focuses on the *speed* of life that you want to live. Space concentrates on creating *margin* in your life so that you have room for interruptions, emergencies, and surprises. Space and Pace work together to protect you from falling back into busyness.

Second, you'll Design your life around **The Core 4**—the four most important characteristics of purposeful, productive, and peaceful people: **Relationships**, **Recreation**, **Rest**, and **Reflection**.

Third, once you've planned for Pace and Space and The Core 4, you can finally begin devising your **Dreams and Priorities**.

You're going to love this step because you get to design the life you want to live! You'll keep Gettin' (un)Busy while accomplishing your Dreams and Priorities.

10

DESIGN PACE AND SPACE

Jerry's assistant notified him of my arrival, and he opened the door to his office. He was wide-eyed, breathless, and looked like he had just seen a ghost. He glanced at me. His eyes darted all around the reception area.

"Come in," he finally said, like a rabbit deciding the area was clear of foxes.

Jerry was the kind of client I like to work with. He cared about both results and relationships. He wanted wanted the whole company to succeed as well as each individual employee. He had hired me to help them develop leaders in his department at a Fortune 500 company. Today, we were pitching our ideas to his peers and supervisor.

When he met me at the door, it appeared as if something terrible had happened. He said, "I know that we have this meeting scheduled, but I need a few more minutes before we can talk. Please wait here, and I'll be back."

I had plenty of time to sit and wonder what was wrong with Jerry. Did the CEO show up unexpectedly? Was Jerry about to get fired? Was he about to fire someone? I wasn't sure what was going on, but I did know that Jerry was a nervous wreck.

Twenty minutes later, Jerry returned.

He didn't greet me. Didn't ask how I was doing. He jumped straight into business. He spoke at a feverish pace. I interrupted him.

"Jerry, what's wrong? What's going on?"

"Oh, everything's fine. I just had an unexpected meeting pop up this morning. It's thrown off my whole day. My schedule was already booked, and now I have to squeeze it all in."

I could tell that Jerry was trapped in the Busyness Vortex – Hurry, Worry, and Scurry.

- **Hurry**—Jerry bobbed and weaved around the office like a boxer in a ring. Words shot out of his mouth. I watched him devour a snack like a starved animal.

- **Worry**—Jerry's anxiety levels were sky-high. Every interaction he had raised everyone else's angst. He was nervous his day wasn't going to go according to plan (which it wasn't) and that he wouldn't get everything finished (which he wouldn't).

- **Scurry**—Jerry couldn't make eye contact with anyone but, like a sentry meerkat, kept looking for signs of danger. His conversation was erratic. He couldn't stay on a single topic for more than a couple of seconds before he started talking about something else.

Have you ever felt like Jerry? You planned your day with every moment filled from start to finish. You started the day wondering how you were going to get it all done. Then, the unexpected happened! You got a flat tire, saw an old friend or had an unscheduled meeting.

I've learned two important lessons. The first is: *no single day goes perfectly according to plan.* Some days are better than others, but you will always have interruptions, emergencies, or surprises. Second, because no day goes perfectly according to plan, *you must design your schedule to account for this reality.*

You make room for the *expected unexpected* by designing the Pace (speed) at which you want to live and Space (margin) in your calendar.

DESIGNING PACE

Over a century ago, European missionaries serving in Africa hired local villagers as porters to help carry supplies to a distant station. For two days, the porters went slower than the missionaries desired. The missionaries determined to push the porters to go faster. On the third day, they doubled their distance. The missionaries congratulated themselves for the increased pace.

But on the fourth day, the porters refused to move. The missionaries asked the porters why they wouldn't budge.

One of the men responded, "We moved so quickly yesterday. We must wait here for our souls to catch up with our bodies."

When I first heard this story many years ago, I thought the porters were lazy. They needed to work harder and faster. However, I've come to realize their wisdom. They intentionally designed the Pace at which they lived.

You can't live with Purpose, Productivity, and Peace if you're moving at a fast, frantic, and fevered pace. The faster your Pace, the more your sympathetic nervous system kicks in. It floods your body with adrenaline and cortisol.

Think about the last time you were late for a meeting. Maybe it took you longer to get ready than you expected or you had a few interruptions from your children. You decided to make up the time by acting like a NASCAR driver.

Can you feel how wide your eyes are? How tight your grip on the steering wheel is? Do you sense how hyper-focused you are as you look for small openings in traffic and for police officers on the side of the road?

Maybe you made it to the meeting on time. But chances are you had already fallen into The Busyness Vortex, and you brought that cycle with you into the meeting.

You short-circuit the Hurry, Worry, Scurry cycle by Designing a slower Pace of life. Choose to live calmly. Talk, walk, eat, read, drive more leisurely. You Design the speed at which you live so that your body doesn't Hurry. When you don't Hurry, you also Worry less. Then you can make better decisions and deal with interruptions, emergencies, and surprises.

As I sat with Jerry in his office, I knew our presentation would crash if he led the meeting while trapped in the Busyness Vortex. Everyone would absorb his worried emotions and attach them to our leadership development solution. I needed to get Jerry calmed down.

I started talking to him very slowly, and I asked him to do the same. When we left his office to go to the meeting room for the presentation, I decelerated my pace so that he had to walk more deliberately. By the time we arrived at the meeting room, Jerry had calmed down. His composure translated into confidence, and the team approved our recommendations.

Design the Pace at which you want to live. Start talking and walking and eating at a unhurried Pace – a peaceful Pace. You'll soon find that Hurry, Worry, and Scurry fade away to be replaced by Purpose, Productivity, and Peace.

DESIGNING SPACE

The financial advisor Dave Ramsey encourages people to build an emergency fund—a six-month reserve of cash in the bank that's set aside just in case a car breaks down or a pipe bursts. Ramsey points out that when you have an emergency fund, you have a lot fewer emergencies.

The same is true when you design Space in your life. Designing Space is like creating a time-based emergency fund.

Busy people like Jerry tend to block every minute of their days. He had filled his calendar with nonstop commitments from seven in the morning till nine at night.

When you fill every minute of the day, you have no room for interruptions, emergencies or surprises, yet the *expected unexpected* happens every single day. You're interrupted when a co-worker pops his head in your cubicle to ask you a "quick question." You have emergencies when your kid gets sick or your car breaks down. You're surprise when you see an old friend at Starbucks.

Interruptions, emergencies, and surprises happen every day, but, if you don't have an emergency time-fund, they will wreck your day and potentially several days. That's why it's vital that you design Space into your schedule.

Here are three simple ways to design Space in everyday life.

1. Carve out fifteen minutes between appointments. You can't be two places at once. That means that you can't end one appointment at 2:00 pm and begin another at the same time. Yet many people schedule their calendars with overlapping engagements.

Instead, carve fifteen minutes between appointments. If you're traveling somewhere, give yourself fifteen minutes extra. This fifteen-minute buffer gives you time to get to the next appointment or allows some margin in case the first appointment goes long.

2. Time-block your priorities. Dave Ramsey also recommends that you build a budget that preallocates your money. Time-blocking means scheduling an appointment with yourself to focus on priorities. If you're preparing for a big presentation, time-block a few hours for research and organization. Block time on your calendar for your workouts. Instead of checking your email throughout the day, schedule three fifteen-minute periods to respond to email.

Time-blocking allows you to predetermine how you're going to spend your time. It protects your time from (un)wanted interruptions because you can tell people, "I can't talk now. I already have an appointment." Time-blocking is a critical practice that I'll come back to several times in this book.

3. Schedule white-space days. About once every four to six weeks, it's wise to schedule a day to catch up on projects or to give yourself a day to slow down. I'm not talking about sitting in your pajamas watching Netflix® all day. White-space days are designed to provide you with time to catch up from interruptions, emergencies, and surprises. When you know a white-space day is already on the calendar, you can rest assured that when something disrupts your schedule, you'll have time later to catch up.

When you Design the Pace at which you live and the Space for the *expected unexpected,* you're on your way to designing the life you want to live. Now, it's time to Design The Core 4.

11

DESIGN THE CORE 4

In my years of research and conversation, I discovered four pillars that are central to people who live with Purpose, Productivity, and Peace. Those four pillars are **Relationships**, **Recreation**, **Rest**, and **Reflection**. I also discovered that *these same four pillars are the first ones busy people sacrifice.* When you become overwhelmed, you're likely to let go of one of these four areas, but when that happens, you not only increase the likelihood of falling back into busyness, you also lose a piece of your humanity.

That's why you must Design The Core 4 into your life. Designing The Core 4 means that you build these four pillars into your schedule *before you schedule anything else.* Most people expect Relationships, Recreation, Rest, and Reflection to happen naturally, so they don't plan for it. Busy people hope The Core 4 will somehow magically fall into their spare time, but there is no spare time.

If you're going to Design the life you want to live, you must lay the foundation of these four pillars before you schedule anything else. Make the rest of your life fit around The Core 4.

Relationships

Before I killed busyness, my family took a weekend retreat to articulate our family purpose and core values. To discover our core values, I asked our kids to share some of the words and phrases our family often repeated. I believed these words and phrases would help us unearth what we valued.

My then six-year-old daughter looked at me and said, "I know something you say a lot, Daddy!" I was thrilled to hear her thoughts. "You say, 'Go! Go! Go!' all the time!" (She widened her eyes and screamed the word "go" to make sure I got her point.)

She was right. My life was so full of good commitments that I had to rush my family out the door every time we went anywhere.

If you had asked me at that time, I would have told you that my relationships with Dorothy and our children were my highest priority. Yet my excess commitments led me to hurry my family around and treat them like cattle to be herded.

You probably became overcommitted because you love other people. In fact, your love of others is one of the most common reasons that busyness happens. It's hard to say *no* to the people you love. However, the busier you get, the more likely it is that you crowd out relationships from your life. You cease to engage in relationships and merely endure them. Eventually, your busyness leads you to push people away.

If you're going to live with Purpose, Productivity, and Peace, you must build relationships into the core of your life. You must Design time around three types of Relationships.

1. Your most important people. To being Designing your life around Relationships, answer the following questions:

- *Who* are the most important people in my life? Is it my spouse? My kids? My parents? A few friends?

- *Where* are the most important people in my life? Are they geographically close, or are they far away?

- *When* can I engage with the most important people in my life?

- *How* can I engage them so that they feel loved and valued?

These are the questions that help you design your life around relationships.

If your most important people are your spouse and kids, you may block from 7-9 pm a few nights every week to spend together. You can schedule a weekly Facetime with your parents who live on the other side of the country. One of my friends has grown children distributed throughout the United States, but every Saturday night, the whole family (including in-laws and grandkids) joins a two-hour conference call to catch everyone up on their weeks.

Reserve time to engage in the most important relationships. There's another kind of relationship to design around.

2. Your most energizing people. Let's be honest. Sometimes the most important people in your life are not the most energizing. Sometimes they're the most exhausting. If you have kids, they may be the most important people to you, but they also may drain you faster than anyone else. Perhaps you have aging parents who require a lot of care. Maybe you love your partner but find participating in activates they enjoy draining. (Which is why they have benches in malls.)

Blocking time for energizing people is critical. What do I mean by energizing people? I'm talking about people who, when you spend time with them, you feel alive, energized and invigorated.

During my quest to get (un)busy, I started having lunch with a group of guys from my church. Bert, Ben, Chad, Josh and I met every Thursday at a Chinese restaurant. We joked around a lot, discussed theology and leadership, and pushed each other to become better husbands, fathers, and leaders. We would hang out for an hour and then all go back to work. After time with them, I felt renewed. I made those lunches a priority because they filled my energy tank for the rest of the week.

Who are the energizing people in your life? How can you begin to spend time with them? If you're going to live with Purpose, Productivity, and Peace, it's critical that you Design your life around these Relationships.

3. Your relationship with God. I believe your most important relationship is with God. You are more than a physical being. Design your life to include time nurturing your spiritual growth. Spiritual practices are vital to living a fulfilling life. Make time to develop a relationship with God by reading sacred literature, practicing silence and meditation, or engaging in prayer.

RECREATION

The second element of The Core 4 is Recreation. *Recreation is any activity that you do for the sheer enjoyment of doing it.*

When I first started talking to Oliver about Recreation, he balked. Even though he had Deconstructed so much busyness from his life, he didn't believe he had time for Recreation. He felt like it was a waste of time. Between his commitments at work and home, how could he find time to do an activity "for the sheer enjoyment of doing it."

Most people believe that they don't have time for Recreation. They think Recreation is unproductive. Dr. Stuart M. Brown, Jr., one of the leading researchers on the effects of play in our lives, disagrees. He writes, "It's paradoxical that a little bit of non-productive activity can make one enormously more productive and invigorated in other aspects of life."[32]

I had to convince Oliver that Recreation is one of the most productive activities in which you can engage. Why? Because *Recreation renews energy.*

You'll never get your time back. Once it's gone, it's gone forever, but energy is renewable. Whether you're at work or running a marathon, you expend vast amounts of energy every day. Then you renew it by eating a good meal or sleeping. Or by engaging in Recreation.

How do you build Recreation into your life? It only takes two simple steps:

1. Identify your play personality.

Brown identifies eight different types of play personality.[33] Understanding your play personality will help you narrow down the types of recreational activities you want to do. Here are the eight play personalities:

1. *The Joker.* For these people, play revolves around non-sense, like a class clown or an adult jokester. They get energy by silliness.

2. *The Kinesthetic.* These people like to move. Many times, they're athletes, dancers, swimmers, or walkers. They often need to move in order to think.

3. *The Explorer.* Explorers never lose their enthusiasm for exploration. It could be exploring new a place, new ideas, new subjects, emotions or points of view. They renew energy by discovering uncharted territory.

4. *The Competitor.* These people are easy to spot. They love activities that involve rules. They want to win. Recreation comes from striving to be the best.

5. *The Director.* These people enjoy planning and executing events or scenes. They love to organize other people. It could be throwing a party or planning a trip or directing a play at the local theater. They want to get people together and do something.

6. *The Collector.* Collectors get energy by gathering an interesting collection of objects or ideas. They want to have and to hold items such as insects, stamps or antiques. They may gather quotes that they find inspiring. Collectors could be solitary, or they could collect with other people.

7. *The Creator.* These people play by making things. They could paint, garden, sculpt or design. They love to take an idea that's in their minds and turn it into something real.

8. *The Storyteller.* Storytellers use their imaginations to create narratives or imaginative worlds. They are quick to tell stories for the entertainment of others or create imaginary situations that add adventure to everyday life.

You probably have multiple play personalities. Determine what type of play personalities you have. If you can't decide, think back to your childhood. What did you do when you were left to yourself to play?

2. Plan your play.

Now that you know your play personality, identify a few options of activities that you would enjoy doing for the sheer enjoyment of doing it. Do you love hiking, watching movies, engaging in deep conversations, building with LEGO® bricks?

Determine some activities that you would enjoy doing, and then block time in your calendar to do it. If you're a Kinesthetic, set aside time to go hiking. If you're a Creator, schedule time to draw or garden. If you're a Director, organize a dinner for people and start inviting them over. Plan your play before you plan your other commitments. Whatever your play personality, schedule Recreation time every day.

Before we move on to **Rest**, I'd like to address a common question: what about exercise? We all know that exercise is important to living a healthy life. I think it's essential to living with Purpose, Productivity, and Peace, but many people see exercise as boring or painful.

My advice is to find a way to make exercise a recreational activity. If you hate running, don't run. But find a way to incorporate exercise using your play personality. Keep trying physical activities until you land on something that brings you to life. Don't be afraid to be the middle-aged participant in the martial arts or Zumba® class!

REST

A friend of mine recently returned from a vacation to Disney World in which his family walked twenty-nine miles in three days. When I asked him if he had taken the time to rest, he replied, "Rest? I'm so exhausted. I need a vacation from my vacation." His time off increased his fatigue rather than his recovery.

Don't get me wrong. I'm all for exciting vacations, but to busy people, *Rest* is a four-letter word that needs to be redeemed.

We are a workaholic society. We deprive ourselves of sleep with 40% of people sleeping less than six hours each night. We work until we're exhausted and consume gallons of caffeine to make it through the day. Toward the end of 2017, 1.1 billion energy drinks were sold every 13 weeks.[34] These energy drinks let us power up instead of resting up.

Not only do we miss out on sleep, but we also sacrifice our vacation time. As I mentioned earlier, from 2000 to 2013, the average number of vacation days that a person took dropped from 21 days per year to 13 days per year. Not only is the number of vacation days decreasing, but, like my friend who went to Disney World, I suspect that the quality of Rest that we get on vacation has also decreased.

Our society treats rest like an enemy to be endured. But in my research, conversations, and my own life, I discovered that those who live with the most Purpose, Productivity, and Peace, treat Rest like a friend to be embraced. They design Rest into their lives and build the remainder of their lives around it.

There are four kinds of Rest humans need to prioritize.

1. Sleep. Honestly, I don't want to write about sleep. For the last decade, it's been studied and written about. Extensive studies have declared that it is critical. For example, the military has analyzed the effects of sleep deprivation on soldiers. "Sleep deprivation doesn't just erode your reflexes, decision-making, and ability to learn; it also has physical effects. Sleep deprivation lowers your immunity and erodes your body's ability to fight off infection."[35]

I don't want to write about sleep because, despite all the research, we continue to ignore it.

I'm not a sleep researcher, but I'd like to summarize all the research I've read so far. Sleep is important. When you sleep, you wash cortisol out of your body. You make better decisions, think more clearly, accomplish more, improve your memory, feel better, keep weight off more easily, and enjoy life more.

So stop treating sleep like an enemy. Intentionally build sleep into your life.

One of the best ways that you can do this is by going to bed at the same time every night. Sleep begins before you fall asleep. It starts when you get into bed.

Many people keep the lights in their rooms on until they feel like they're ready to fall asleep. Start turning off the lights at the same time every night. You'll soon find that you fall asleep more quickly and experience better sleep.

2. Naps. Winston Churchill was famous for the midday naps that he took during World War II. Let that sink in for a moment. During a devastating war, this critical leader daily tucked himself away for some slumber.

A short nap of twenty minutes can restore energy and boost your ability to concentrate. While as-needed naps can benefit you, you can see even better results from time-blocking a regular nap into your life.

My mother was a teacher at the school I attended. Each day, we would ride home together. As soon as we got home, she would put on her pajamas, close the door to her room, and take a 15-20-minute nap. I thought it was a strange habit until I got to college.

I did not have great sleep habits in college, but I started taking naps—sometimes multiple naps—each day. I discovered that a 20-minute nap gave me the energy and mental clarity to continue studying (or procrastinate studying with more social activities).

Sleep researcher Sara Mednick discovered that well-timed naps can benefit you physically, mentally, and increase your creativity. "About six hours after you wake up, your body's circadian rhythm starts to dip and you're likely to feel drowsy, especially if you've had a busy morning and lunch. A twenty-minute power nap at this point (say at 1:00 pm) is enough to give you a mental recharge without leaving you groggy: if you keep it short, you'll wake up fairly alert and can quickly get back to work."[36]

3. Stopping. Design times in your life to stop striving and working. A few weeks ago, my entire family spent a Saturday engaging in a "Stop Day."

The previous eight weeks had involved visiting with friends and family every weekend. I had traveled with work more than usual during that time, and we were still trying to get settled into our new house.

As Dorothy and I were planning the weekend, we paid attention to how our bodies felt. We were tired. We determined that we needed to stop, so we declared Saturday a Stop Day.

We made some simple crockpot soup, watched college football, played games, took naps. If you look at our checklist, it would appear we accomplished nothing that weekend, but the stop was exactly what we needed. It resupplied our energy reserves.

There are times that you need to intentionally stop. You can plan this on a weekly basis (more on this when I talk about stopping for one day every week), or you can build a stop day into your calendar at the end of every quarter.

4. Mental Rest. The average person makes dozens of decisions every day.[37] You decide what you're going to wear, what you're going to eat, how you're going to spend your time, etc. All this decision making results in a condition known as "decision fatigue." You've probably experienced this when you say to yourself, "I just can't make another decision today."

Because decision fatigue is a reality for busy people, it's crucial that you build mental Rest into your life. How can you do this? Here are a few suggestions.

- Commit to less. You already started this in the Deconstruction step, but keep committing to (un) commit. The fewer commitments you have, the fewer decisions you make.

- Delegate decision-making responsibilities to others.

- Take decision breaks. Instead of deciding what your family will eat every night, pick one night each week when everyone decides for themselves and makes their own dinner. You could also assign each member of your family one night of the week to plan the menu. We have found children are able to participate in simple meal preparation as early as kindergarten. Most busy parents wait to hand off responsibilities because it takes time to teach kids cook. Yet it pay dividends when they can take on the extra responsibility.

- Set time limits on how long you'll take to decide. The longer you spend thinking about a decision, the more exhausting the decision becomes. Limit the amount of time you spend on decisions. For example, when you're deciding on Christmas presents for your extended family, set a thirty-minute limit to look at Amazon.com. Strive to make all your decisions in that time, or you'll have to come back another day.

Rest may be a four-letter word to busy people. But if you want to live with Purpose, Productivity, and Peace, make Rest part of your life every day.

REFLECTION

The final pillar of The Core 4 is Reflection. Reflection often gets bad press from busy people. They have a mental image of old people sitting with legs crossed and chanting *ohm* as they try to figure out the meaning of life. Others think of Reflection as introspective navel-gazing. Busy people don't have time for either of those.

When I talk about Reflection, I'm thinking of a championship football team. Championship teams review game film so that they can capitalize on their strengths, examine and correct their mistakes, and play better during the next game. In the same way, Reflection is looking back so that you can move forward.

Busy people don't take time to reflect. They stay focused on what's directly in front of them. However, if you want to Design your life so that you can live with Purpose, Productivity, and Peace, you must look back so that you can move forward.

I recommend having both daily and weekly Reflection, both of which can be done in a few minutes.

Daily Reflection. Daily Reflection should only take two minutes per day. Do it at the end of the day by answering three questions:

- *What did I accomplish today?* Busy people tend to see only the things that they didn't accomplish rather than all the things they did. I find it helpful to look back on what I accomplished and to celebrate those victories.

- *What am I grateful for today?* Create a gratitude list. It could include a conversation you had with a friend, or maybe your biggest accomplishment of the day. This little act can have huge benefits: "When researchers pick random volunteers and train them to be more grateful over a period of a few weeks, they become happier and more optimistic, feel more socially connected, enjoy better quality sleep, and even experience fewer headaches than control groups."[38]

- *What will I do differently?* This question helps you reflect on mistakes you can correct and improvements you can make in the future. Did you let yourself get caught up in Hurry, Worry, and Scurry? Did you fail to build margin into your life? Did you speak harshly to someone? Only by looking back can you correct those mistakes in the future.

Weekly Reflection. Your Weekly Reflection looks similar but still only takes about ten minutes. Ask yourself three questions.

- What did I accomplish last week?

- What am I grateful for from the last week?

- What will I do differently?

If you're wondering about looking ahead and planning, we'll cover that when I introduce you to Preflection in Chapter 14.

These pillars—Relationships, Recreation, Rest, and Reflection—make up The Core 4. Busy people try to fit these into the nooks and crannies of their lives, but you're going to live differently. You're going to live with Purpose, Productivity, and Peace. To do that, you start your Design with the pillars of The Core 4. Build everything else around them. Do it now! Before you move to the next chapter, pull out your calendar and block time for Relationships, Recreation, Rest, and Reflection.

When you've done that, it will be time to take the final step in your Design: Design your Dreams and Priorities.

12

DESIGN YOUR DREAMS AND PRIORITIES

For a couple of years, my family lived in a suburb of Houston, Texas. While we loved our friends there, we were frustrated and discontent with almost every other area of life. My job wasn't what I expected it to be. We were uncomfortable in our house and neighborhood. We weren't thrilled with our kids' schools. We knew that our family needed a change, so we started talking about me looking for a new job.

However, there was something more important than me finding a job. We had a Dream. For years, Dorothy and I had talked about moving to East Tennessee. We loved the natural beauty of the area and were drawn to the Smoky Mountains where we had lived in our younger years. We particularly liked Knoxville, a moderately-sized city with the friendliness of a small town. For years, we had talked about retiring there, but Tennessee always seemed like a far-away dream.

So, we made a crazy decision. We decided to stop looking for a job and start turning our Dream of Tennessee into a Priority.

What is the difference between Dreams and Priorities? *Dreams are long-term desires without a plan or a deadline. Priorities are Dreams that you are willing to sacrifice for and that you have turned into a plan with a deadline.*

Busy people have Dreams, but they don't have time to turn their Dreams into Priorities and their Priorities into reality. They have so many commitments that they go through the motions of life and miss out on the life they want to live.

But you're taking the steps to get (un)busy. The result is that you'll have more time, energy, and attention to give to your biggest Dreams and highest Priorities. Now that you've made it this far, it's time to start Designing your life so *your* Dreams can become Priorities and your Priorities can become your reality.

How do you Design Space for Dreams and Priorities? Six steps will help you identify your Dreams, turn them into Priorities, and act on those Priorities every day.

1. Write down your Dreams.

Start by writing down your Dreams. Remember, your *Dreams are long-term desires that you have without a plan or a deadline.* Don't just keep these Dreams trapped in your mind. That's what busy people do. They have Dreams and desires, but they don't take the time to write them down.

Writing down your Dreams lets you see them all in one place. You can compare your Dreams, see how they connect and overlap. You can review them regularly to see how they change and update them with new Dreams.

So, write them down. I use a mind-mapping program to capture my Dreams based on several categories: personal growth, health, family, career, influence, finances, experiences, and travel. But it's just as effective to capture your Dreams on a word processor or in your favorite journal.

2. Every ninety days, select two to four Priorities.

Once you have your Dreams captured, it's time to determine your Priorities. Remember, Priorities are Dreams that you are willing to sacrifice for and that you have turned into a plan with a deadline.

First, select no more than four Priorities, preferably less. A lot of people push back at the low number. When you write down all your Dreams, it's natural to want to make them all happen as soon as you can.

However, the smaller the number of Priorities, the higher the likelihood of success. Priorities tend to absorb significant amounts of time, energy, and attention. The more Priorities you have, the less focused you can be on each of them, so select the smallest number possible. I like to remind my clients: *you can prioritize anything you want, but you can't do everything at once.*

Second, update or select new Priorities every ninety days. Research has shown that most people can only maintain focus for about ninety days.[39] Learn to "chunk down" your Dreams into ninety-day Priorities. Some of your Dreams may take longer than that, but you can break it down into smaller pieces.

For example, with our move to Tennessee, we had a Dream of moving there and getting settled. It took ninety days for me to find a job opportunity that could locate us in Tennessee. It took another ninety days to sell and pack up our house in Texas and find a house in Tennessee. It took another ninety days to move, register vehicles, unpack boxes, register our kids for school and get somewhat settled.

Update your Priorities every ninety days so you can stay focused and keep moving forward.

Third, write down your Priorities. Just like with your Dreams, write your Priorities down so you can own them and review them regularly.

I've found a simple formula for writing Priorities to be very effective:

From X to Y by When.[40]

Write each Priority in a statement that identifies *your current reality* (X), *your desired reality* (Y), and *the date it will be accomplished* (When).

- Sell and move out of our house in Texas and move into a new home in Tennessee by August 1.

- Go from talking about a vacation to planning one (including dates, tickets, and hotel reservations) by February 15.

- Advance from running a 5k to completing a half-marathon by November 15.

3. Determine what's not a Priority.

Busy people identify Priorities and then try to pack them into their already overloaded lives. Cramming in your Priorities is a recipe for failure. Instead, determine anything that's not a Priority.

One of my Dreams has been to write this book. It signed with my publisher in August 2017 to make it happen. I had hoped to have it produced by the end of the following year, but by October, moving to Tennessee became our family's top Priority. I knew that I couldn't teach about Gettin' (un)Busy and trap myself in it by writing a book while moving across the country. I determined that moving was a higher Priority than the book. So, I put the book on hold for nearly nine months.

4. Block time for your Priorities. Every. Single. Day.

Time-blocking is critical for turning your Priorities into reality. First, block time on your calendar for The Core 4. Then block your Priorities and build the rest of life around them.

Make time every day to work on your Priorities, even if it's just a few minutes. Your Priorities will be the easiest thing to procrastinate because they're often intimidating and may seem far-off and nonurgent. Develop the habit of making small progress on your Priorities every day. Over time, small wins can add up to huge victories.

5. Track your progress.

I remember the first few days of a new school year always felt overwhelming. For every new class I attended, the instructor handed out a syllabus. As I looked at everything that I needed to accomplish in the next few months, I experienced "syllabus shock." I saw all the impending reading, papers, and tests and nearly had a nervous breakdown.

That's how Priorities can feel.

During my master's education, I finally learned to break down all my assignments and put them in a task management system. I could see my task list diminish every day as I moved closer to the end of the semester. This little act of tracking my progress kept me focused on what I needed to do and let me celebrate what I accomplished every day.

Track your progress so you can celebrate your advancement of turning Priorities into reality. Hint: you can track your progress easily during your Daily Reflection when you ask the first question: *What did I accomplish today?*

6. Review and update your Dreams and Priorities every ninety days.

Finally, schedule time every ninety days to review and update your Dreams and Priorities. Schedule two hours to go back through your Dreams list. Has anything changed? Do you need to delete a Dream because it no longer applies? Do you need to add any Dreams? Do any of your Dreams rise to the top as something to prioritize for the next Quarter?

I love seeing people like you get (un)busy. Not simply because I believe that busyness is killing you, but also—and more importantly—because I get to see people discover their Dreams and turn those into Priorities. When you're stressed, exhausted, and overwhelmed, you only have enough time and energy for everyone else's Priorities. But, when you get (un)busy, you can design your Dreams and Priorities into your life to make them a reality.

I know this personally. I'm typing this manuscript in my home office in Knoxville, Tennessee. At least once a week, Dorothy and I venture into our beloved Smoky Mountains for a hike. Both the home and the book were long-time Dreams that became Priorities, and those Priorities have become reality. It all started with Deciding to get (un)busy; then Deconstructing the beliefs, habits and commitments that kept me trapped in busyness; and then Designing life so that our Dreams and Priorities could happen.

Now that you've done the Design, it's time to Develop your calendar, mind, and habits to help you maximize your Purpose, Productivity, and Peace.

STEP 3: GET BUSY GETTIN' (UN)BUSY

It's time to begin Designing the life you want to live. Most people jump straight into identifying their Dreams and Priorities, but that's a recipe for busyness. First, Design the Pace and Space of life you want. Second, Design your life around the four pillars of an (un)busy life: Relationships, Recreation, Rest, and Reflection. Then, Design your life to accomplish your Dreams and Priorities.

DESIGN PACE AND SPACE

Because no day goes perfectly according to your plan, you must Design your schedule to account for this reality. Account for this reality by designing the Pace (speed) at which you want to live and Space (margin) in your calendar.

- ☐ Start talking, walking, and eating more slowly. By slowing down your body, you short-circuit the Busyness Vortex of Hurry, Worry, and Scurry.

- ☐ Create Space in your life by adding fifteen minutes of margin between appointments.

- ☐ Time-block your Priorities to preallocate time.

- ☐ Schedule white-space days every four to six weeks to catch up on projects or slow down.

DESIGN THE CORE 4

Four pillars are central to living with Purpose, Productivity, and Peace: Relationships, Recreation, Rest, and Reflection. You must Design your life around these pillars.

- ☐ Determine who your most important and most energizing people are and block time to spend with them.

- ☐ Determine your play personality, then Plan Your Play by blocking time for recreational activities.

- ☐ Schedule time for sleep, naps, stopping, and mental rest.

- ☐ Make time in your calendar for Daily and Weekly Reflection.

DESIGN YOUR DREAMS AND PRIORITIES

Busy people have Dreams, but they don't have time to turn their Dreams into Priorities and their Priorities into reality. They have so many commitments that they go through the motions of life and miss out on the life they want to live.

Gettin' (un)Busy frees up time for your biggest Dreams and highest Priorities. Dreams are long-term desires without a plan or a deadline. Priorities are Dreams you are willing to sacrifice for and that you have turned into a plan with a deadline.

- ☐ Write down your Dreams.

- ☐ Every ninety days select two to four Priorities.

- ☐ Determine what's not a Priority.

- ☐ Block time for your Priorities every day.

- ☐ Track your progress.

- ☐ Review and update your Dreams and Priorities every ninety days.

STEP 4

DEVELOP

Imagine that you're building the house of your dreams. You would go through several stages. First, you would decide you were ready to build it. Then, you would pick out the land and have it cleared (deconstruction). Third, you would work with an architect to design your house. Then, you would start the most exciting step—development. You would get to experience your ideas turn into reality. You would watch the frame go up, the roof, the walls, and the flooring.

Every time I've talked to someone who's built a house, they say the development phase is the most exciting.

The same is true in your journey to get (un)busy. You've been doing a lot of hard work to prepare for the new life that you want to live. You Decided to get (un)busy. You Deconstructed beliefs, habits, and commitments that kept you trapped. You finished the Design step where you created Space and Pace for The Core 4 and for your biggest Dreams and Priorities. Now it's time for the Develop step, which is where you'll introduce new ways of living that will keep you from falling back into busyness.

However, this step will do more than that. You'll Develop a calendar, mindset, and habits that will help you live with greater Purpose, Productivity, and Peace. To make it simpler, I'll call these your (un)Busy Calendar, (un)Busy Mind, and (un)Busy Habits.

13

DEVELOP AN (UN)BUSY CALENDAR

The first time Oliver talked to me about his exhaustion and busyness, he pulled out his tablet and showed me his calendar. Every space was filled. Even worse, his calendar didn't include all the interruptions at the office or responsibilities at home.

Oliver, like most people, thought that the key to beating busyness was implementing better time management, and, like most people, he believed one solution was to have a well-organized calendar.

As you've seen by now, we've largely ignored your calendar as you've been going through the process of Gettin' (un)Busy. Your calendar has two fundamental flaws. That is why I have ignored it until this point.

(1) *Your calendar is only as helpful as you are disciplined.* If you don't write down the commitments you make, you'll miss your appointments, and your calendar will do no good.

(2) *Your calendar only records your best guess as to how your commitments will go.* You can fill your calendar with your appointments, but it is, at best, a predictive guess

as to how your day will go. Have you ever been to a doctor's office that took ninety minutes more than you expected?

Managing your time and calendar are never the problem with busyness, which is why we've largely ignored your calendar until now.

Now that you've gone through the first three steps, it's time to update the way you manage your calendar. Four best practices will help you manage your calendar.

1. Change the way you think about your calendar.

Up until this point, you've probably thought of a calendar very reactively. When someone asks another person to do something, the invitee's calendar acts as a tool to help them respond. They pull out their calendar, look to see if they have availability, and then say yes. This habit is what busy people do, and it's the wrong way to think about your calendar.

Instead, *your calendar is a tool for proactively organizing your life for Purpose, Productivity, and Peace.* Let me explain.

- Your calendar is a tool. Just like a hammer or a screwdriver, your calendar is a tool to be used for a specific purpose.

- Your calendar's purpose is to organize your life proactively. You are the steward of your own time. Only you can give it away. Take responsibility for it by putting your most important Priorities and commitments into your calendar first and building everything else around those.

Your calendar should result in Purpose, Productivity, and Peace. When you take responsibility for your calendar, you determine how you spend your time. You choose the Pace at which you live. If someone asks you to do something that doesn't line up with your Priorities, you have the power to say *no*! You organize your time so that you live with Purpose, Productivity, and Peace.

2. Block your Core 4, Priorities and Boundaries.

I've already shown you the importance of time-blocking your Core 4 and Priorities. Do this on a weekly basis.

Additionally, put your End-of-Work and End-of-Day Boundaries in your calendar. I've found that this helps you see your boundaries as commitments that need to be honored. Set an alarm to go off fifteen minutes before each boundary in your calendar. This reminder notifies you that the Boundary is approaching and allows you to finish up your task.

3. Manage Your Margin

When you Designed your Pace and Space, I introduced you to the concept of Margin. I told you to give yourself time in between commitments because you can't stop one commitment and start another at the same time.

Take proactive responsibility for your calendar by giving yourself Margin. If it takes thirty minutes to get to your office, block forty minutes. Because I've never had a doctor's appointment end early, I've started blocking three hours in my calendar. That gives me plenty of Margin.

There's another way you can Manage Your Margin. Before you start each week, glance over your calendar and see if there are any areas in which you have overlapping appointments. When you find them, change your calendar to give yourself time between them. If an appointment includes others, send them a quick email saying, "We need to end this meeting at 4:45 instead of 5:00."

Manage your **Margin** to give yourself Space for the unexpected.

4. Stop one day every week.

This practice may be one of the most challenging things that I ask you to do. It was challenging and uncomfortable for me when Dorothy asked me to do it.

I had started working on my master's degree. Every week, I had hundreds of pages to read, two new languages to learn, and dozens of pages to write. I also aspired to earn a doctorate, so I made it my goal to have a 3.75 GPA. When you combine my love of learning with a competitive nature and workaholic tendencies, school was an obsession waiting to happen.

Dorothy knew me well enough to know that I would over-indulge to school. That's when she asked me to do something very uncomfortable. She asked me to take one day off every week. She asked me to take a Sabbath.

In the Judeo-Christian tradition, Sabbath is a twenty-four-hour period in which no work is to take place. Sabbath is included in the Ten Commandments that God gave to the Israelites. Like the other commandments, Sabbath was intended to be a best-living practice. The Creator was giving insight to his creation on how he designed them to optimally function.

But when Dorothy asked me to take a Sabbath, I was horrified and scared. How could I complete all my work in only six days each week? I was confident that she was sabotaging my education and destroying any chance of me getting into a doctoral program. I reluctantly agreed, but I was ready to blame her for my failure.

Instead of failing, though, I flourished. When my class-mates arrived on Mondays, they looked exhausted, but I was filled with energy and enthusiasm. Many classmates lost momentum as the semester progressed. Some of them even dropped out. I gained momentum.

As I saw the gap between my classmates and me in energy and enthusiasm, I realized that Dorothy hadn't sabotaged my education. She had enhanced it. However, I didn't get a 3.75 GPA; I earned a 3.96.

When my master's program ended, so did the practice of this day off. The next eight years brought changes that I've already detailed, (long work hours, three children, a doctoral program) and all of that brought busyness.

As Dorothy and I became overwhelmed by all the good commitments we made, we redetermined to take one day off from all forms of work every week. We believed from experience that it would work, but it felt counterintuitive. It seemed like the opposite of what we needed to do. How in the world could taking one day off every week help us become less busy?

Oliver thought the same thing. He said, "I have more to do than I can get done in seven days. You're telling me that I should try to cram everything into six? You're crazy!"

I asked him to try it out for two months. Taking one day off every week is a big risk, but I've found that taking a weekly Sabbath is one of the most powerful secret ingredients of living with Purpose, Productivity, and Peace.

In fact, I've discovered that Sabbath makes you *more* productive. Here's how.

1. Sabbath reenergizes you. When you fully disengage from all work, you refill your energy, which fuels you for the next week.

2. Sabbath gives you more time. Remember Parkinson's law? *Work expands to fill the time allotted.* If you shrink the amount of time that you give to work, the work shrinks to fill the time.

3. Sabbath provides Space for The Core 4. Sabbath gives you Space to engage in Relationships, Recreation, Rest, and Reflection.

4. Sabbath is a reward to anticipate. When you know that there's a reward coming, you will work harder and smarter. Allow Sabbath to be something to look forward to.

How to take a Sabbath

In my small e-book *Take 52 Days Off This Year and Get More Done*, I give step-by-step guidance for taking a Sabbath by the end of the week. It takes less than one hour to read and has helped many people take a Sabbath. You can get a copy of the book at **www.gettinunbusybook.com/SabbathBook**

Space doesn't permit me to share all the ideas from that book, but I will share four steps that will help you take a Sabbath.

1. Pick the twenty-four hours you will take off.

You will never slip into Sabbath. You must be intentional. Select the hours in advance. For most people, I recommend starting on Saturday evening and ending on Sunday evening.

2. Determine what you WON'T do.

Certain activities are work for you. Avoid these activities during your Sabbath. For me, it's email, house cleaning, and yard work. Commit to yourself that you won't do any of those activities during your one day off each week.

3. Determine what you WILL do.

I think it's wise to determine how you will spend your day off. Sabbath isn't a day of waste. It's a day of replenishment. You don't have to plan out your entire Sabbath, but identify the types of activities that you will do or would like to do.

Do you want to read? Cook? Worship? Spend time with friends? Go on a hike? Journal? Take a nap?

Refer to your Play Personality. Select several types of activities that you want to do. These give you options of ways to spend your twenty-four hours of Sabbath.

4. Build a startup and shutdown ritual.

One of the best practices is to have an easy, specific ritual that helps mark off your Sabbath. You could pray at the beginning and end of Sabbath. You could gather your family together for a Sabbath commencement celebration. You could have a Sabbath candle that you light at the beginning and extinguish at the end.

You need something that puts a stake in the ground to say, "the next twenty-four hours are different than usual."

Oliver tried out Sabbath for eight weeks. The first few weeks were hard. He felt guilty for stopping when he had so much to do at work and home. But after a few weeks, he started noticing his renewed energy. His family got their chores done by Saturday morning so they could feel free to start their Sabbath on Saturday evening. They blocked off time after Sabbath on Sunday night to tie up loose ends and prepare for the upcoming week.

After the eight weeks, I asked Oliver if he was going to stop Sabbath. "I'll never go back to working seven days! I'm getting more accomplished than ever before, and I've got more energy."

Your calendar is a tool that can help you proactively organize your life for Purpose, Productivity, and Peace. It's time to take control of it.

14

DEVELOP AN (UN)BUSY MIND

One of my favorite Disney movies is *Up*, which includes a talking and lovable—but not too bright—dog named Dug.

In the scene where we meet Dug, he introduces himself to the main character, "My name is Dug. I have just met you, and I love you. My master made me this collar. He is a good and smart master, and he made me this collar so that I may talk."

Suddenly, Dug's eyes widen, and he looks to the side. "SQUIRREL!"

After a long pause, Dug returns to his conversation, "My master is good and smart."

Dug, along with the bad talking dogs, is on a mission to find a large bird. Throughout the movie, they get distracted when they sense a squirrel is around. They suffer from a condition that I refer to as "Squirrel Brain."

When you get trapped in busyness, you develop a case of Squirrel Brain.

- You can't focus for more than a few minutes on your most important Priorities. SQUIRREL!

- You allow constant interruptions into your day. SQUIRREL!

- You get distracted by text messages and notifications when you're spending time with the most important people in your life. SQUIRREL!

- You're thinking about all the things that you need to do instead of what you're doing. SQUIRREL!

At the end of *Up*, the bad talking dogs are defeated when one of the main characters screams "Squirrel!" The dogs get distracted from their mission and crash their airplanes. (It's a Disney movie, so it makes sense that talking dogs are also flying planes.)

Squirrel Brain caused their defeat, and it can defeat you from your mission to get (un)busy.

Your mind is one of your most essential tools against busyness. If it's constantly distracted and unfocused, you will fall back into busyness. Fight against Squirrel Brain by developing an (un)busy mind. In order to do this, you need to learn a few practices.

PRACTICE #1: WRITE IT DOWN

Have you ever had this experience: You are at work, concentrating on a critical project. Suddenly, you remember that you need to pick up milk and eggs on your way home. You push the thought to the back of your mind and get back to work. Throughout the rest of the day, you remember thirty more times that you need to pick up milk and eggs. You tell yourself that there's no way you can forget to stop by the store. But, somehow, you forget to pick up milk and eggs on your way home. (Of course, I'm not speaking from experience…)

Busy people keep their thoughts, ideas, and actions trapped inside their minds. But this habit leads to several problems.

First, when you fail to get these distractions out of your head, you create mental congestion. Thoughts, ideas, and actions clog up your mind by fighting for your attention with "pop-up" notifications.

Second, when you hold everything inside, you diminish your ability to engage in the big Priorities that demand your best attention. Your mind can only give *concentrated* focus to one thing at a time. It is possible for you to do a mindless activity (e.g., cleaning up from dinner) while simultaneously doing something that requires concentration (e.g., listening to an audiobook). But it's not possible for you to give concentrated focus to more than one thing at a time. If you try to listen to an audiobook while learning how to play the tuba, you won't do either well.

Third, you use your brain for remembering, *instead of* thinking. Remembering is about storing information. Your brain is ill-equipped for storage. Try to remember all of your friends' birthdays. You may be able to recollect a few, but certainly not all of them, because your mind is abysmal at remembering.

Your brain is not designed to *remember* when all of your friends were born. Its function is to *think* about special ways to celebrate your friends' birthdays. Your brain was made for thinking: problem-solving, planning, and creating.

Fourth, keeping all your thoughts, ideas, and actions inside your head increases your anxiety. With the new spark of an idea in your mind comes the compulsion to ignite it immediately. You start feeling tension between what you're doing and what you're thinking about.

Busy people operate by keeping their thoughts in their head. But (un)busy people develop the habit of writing things down. They create mental space by getting everything out of their heads and into a trusted system. Develop the habit of writing things down so your brain will stop reminding you of all the things you're not doing. You'll discover a more Peace-filled life.

You can get everything out of your mind by developing the practice of *writing it down.* Here's how.

1. Do a brain dump.

Spend fifteen minutes clearing everything out of your mind. Write down (or type out) everything that comes to your mind that you need to do or remember.

Do you need to get a card for Aunt Sally's birthday? Write it down.

Are you supposed to get cash for your kid's field trip? Write it down.

Do you have a book that you want to read and need to order it? Write it down.

Get everything out of your mind as quickly as you can.

2. Take a note-taking tool with you everywhere.

Take something with you everywhere to get things out of your mind. Your thoughts will occur in random places. Make sure you have a method for capturing those thoughts as they arise.

It can be paper or digital. But if you choose digital, there are two pieces of advice to follow: (1) Use the same program every time; (2) Select a program that lets you capture the thought quickly. If it takes too many steps to capture the idea, you'll forget it while you navigate to the program.

Take something with you EVERYWHERE.

3. Take ten minutes each day to process what you captured.

At some point each day, process all the reminders and to-do items that you've captured. I process mine just before the end of the workday. When you process the action, take one of four actions:

(1) Delete it. Just because you captured something doesn't mean you must do it. You'll be less busy if you delete it.

(2) Delegate it. Can you assign this task to one of your direct reports or ask someone else to do this for you? If possible, give it away.

(3) Do it. If it will only take a few minutes to do, go ahead and do it.

(4) Defer it. If you can't do it right away, add it to your calendar or to-do list. That way, you don't have to remember it.

PRACTICE #2: ACCEPT YOUR CONSTRAINTS

Mary had dreams of writing a novel and becoming a published author. She did the hard work of Gettin' (un)Busy and freed up significant amounts of time to turn this Dream into a Priority.

After three months of intense writing, she got the news that her aging parents were struggling to live by themselves. Her mother kept falling, and her father didn't have the strength to help her up. Mary weighed her options and decided it would be best for her parents to move in with her family.

Her writing slowed down dramatically. Mary helped her parents get settled and spent more time giving them the attention they needed. But she grew frustrated as her writing Priority faded deeper into the distance. The more frustrated she became, the harder it was to write. When she was helping her parents, she felt guilty for not writing; when she was writing, she felt guilty for not paying attention to her parents. When she called me for coaching, we identified the problem as an unwillingness to accept her constraints.

Everyone has constraints. A constraint is simply a limitation. You have limits on your time, energy, attention, and finances. Your job creates constraints. It may dictate where you live, when you work, or how often you go on vacation. Whether or not you have a job, your relationships create constraints. Having a family may put career aspirations on hold. Your money may go toward kids' braces instead of an anniversary trip. You may have a friend who is diagnosed with cancer and needs your help. Your children's activities take up evening hours.

Busyness often emerges when you try to deny the reality of your constraints and cram more commitments into your life. Mary was doing this. She denied how much effort it took to care for her parents. She wanted to write at the same intense speed as she had been before they moved in.

There are two types of constraints in your life: Movable and (un)Movable. **Movable Constraints** are the limitations you can change. In the Deconstruct step, you eliminated Movable Constraints. You got rid of unnecessary commitments. You delegated projects that were constraining you. Movable Constraints are easy to get rid of if you don't want them.

(un)Movable Constraints are those limitations you cannot change, but there are two types of (un)Movable Constraints: *Imposed* and *Chosen.*

1. *Imposed, (un)Movable Constraints* are the limitations you didn't choose but are part of your life. You have a special needs child who requires extra attention. Your loved one dies suddenly, leaving you to settle his estate. Your boss expects you to work a long weekend to fix a problem that's causing problems for your customers. You may not have chosen this path, but these are *Imposed, (un)Movable Constraints.*

2. *Chosen, (un)Movable Constraints* are those limits that you wanted and that you do not wish to move. They are the constraints created by choosing something as a Priority. Mary experienced this kind of constraint with her parents. She *could* have sent them to a nursing home, but she believed it was best for them to live with her. She chose this as a constraint, and she was not willing to move it.

How do you deal with each of these constraints?

- If it's a *Movable Constraint*, you decide if you want to release yourself from it. If so, you commit to (un) commit.

- If it's an *Imposed, (un)Movable Constraint*, you simply must accept the constraint.

- If it's a *Chosen, (un)Movable Constraint*, you must decide: do you want to release yourself from it? If so, commit to (un)commit. If not, accept the constraint.

But how do you accept your constraints?

1. Acknowledge reality.

When Mary and I first started talking, she said several times, "If only they didn't require so much care, I could spend more time on writing." These two little words – *if only* – will shut down your mind.

- If only I had more money…

- If only I had more time…

- If only I could quit my job…

- If only I didn't have to take care of my parents…

These two words kill your Dreams and Priorities. They distract you from reality and focus your attention on a fictionalized version of your life. "Speaking these words preoccupies us with either the future or the past. It assures us that our happiness lies in those places that implicitly define our present life by what is missing."[41]

Acknowledge the reality that these constraints are part of your life. Whether they've been Imposed or Chosen, they are part of your life. Stop focusing on "if only" and accept your present reality.

2. Surrender to your constraints.

Now that you've acknowledged it, accept it. You can try to reject it, but it won't do you any good. Accept that this is a constraint.

Mary didn't need to merely acknowledge that her parents took time and attention from her writing. She needed to surrender to the reality that she had less time for writing. She needed to stop trying to fight it and learn to accept it.

3. DETERMINE WHAT YOU CAN DO.

I helped Mary brainstorm some possibilities of what she could do. She made two commitments. First, she would write at least 1,000 words every day. Second, she told her parents that unless they had an emergency, she needed to work from 9-11 am every day.

You don't have unlimited resources in pursuing your Dreams and Priorities, but you can do *something*. Figure out what you can do so that you can take action.

It took longer than she wanted, but Mary finally published her book. She also took care of her parents well in the last years of their lives. It all started with accepting her constraints.

PRACTICE #3: REFLECT AND PREFLECT

In Reflection (the fourth pillar of The Core 4), you learned a simple process for looking back at your days and weeks to look ahead to the future.

Now it's time to supplement Reflection with Preflection.

Preflection is the act of looking ahead and determining what you want or need to do in the coming days and weeks.

It's looking at the commitments you have and the Priorities you want to give time to.

If Reflection was looking at the "previous game's film" to see how you did, Preflection is looking at the next opponent's game film to see what you're facing. However, I don't want you to think of the next week as your opponent but as your opportunity. The next week is your opportunity to bring your Priorities closer to reality. It's your opportunity to live with Purpose, Productivity, and Peace.

Preflection involves looking at and answering five questions:

1. What is coming up?

Look at your calendar (and your project list if you have one) for the next couple of weeks. What are your appointments? Do you have a big deadline that requires attention? Are there special dates (birthdays, anniversaries) that need planning?

2. Do I have time blocked for The Core 4?

As you look at your calendar, make sure that it reflects your commitment to Relationships, Recreation, Rest, and Reflection. Do you have time blocked in your calendar for each of these to happen? What do you need to move to take time for The Core 4?

3. What *could* I do?

Once you know what your commitments are, list out all the things that you could do at work and in your personal life. Take a sheet of paper and divide it into two columns, one personal and one work. Brain dump all the possible projects and tasks that you could do in the week ahead so that you can see your options.

4. What *should* I do?

Once you've made time for your Core 4, know what commitments already exist, and think about your other possibilities, answer the question, "What *should* I do?" This question helps you identify what you believe you need to do. I put a small mark by each of these to help me identify them as having a higher Priority.

5. What three *must* I do?

If you've learned anything by now in this book, it's that busyness comes about from an overcommitment to too many good commitments. It's easy to look at all these tasks you *could* and *should* do and think that you *must* do all of them, but that will lead you straight back to busyness.

That's why the last question limits you to three. How do you do this? At the beginning of the week, think ahead to the end of the week. Ask yourself, *When I get to the end of the week, what are the three most important things I will have accomplished?* Write them down. Commit to doing them. Then block time to get them done.[42]

It's that simple. But it's a powerful weapon to help you accomplish your Dreams and live with greater Purpose, Productivity, and Peace.

There are three more insights that can help you with Reflection and Preflection:

1. You can do your Reflection and Preflection at the same time or separately. That's your choice. My brain needs to separate the two, so I make sure there's a small gap between Reflection and Preflection.

2. Do Reflection and Preflection both daily and weekly. This practice helps align daily commitments with weekly Priorities.

3. Time-block your daily and weekly Reflection and Preflection. Schedule time for this to happen so it doesn't fall through the cracks.

Don't let Squirrel Brain cause you to slip back into busyness. Your mind is one of the most important tools in your fight for Purpose, Productivity, and Peace. Develop an (un)busy mind by writing it all down, accepting your constraints, and practicing Reflection and Preflection.

15

DEVELOP (UN)BUSY HABITS

C harles Duhigg's masterful book, *The Power of Habits*, claims that your habits comprise nearly 40-45% of your life.[43] These habits, when added together, shape, and in many ways, determine the course of your life. So, getting your habits right is critical. As you move away from busyness, develop habits that will help you live with greater Purpose, Productivity, and Peace.

Three habits will enable you to live an (un)busy life. First, develop a peace-filled morning routine. Second, tame the transitions that occur throughout your day so that you don't fall into Hurry, Worry, and Scurry. Lastly, build systems for your repeatable tasks and projects so you can save time and energy.

HABIT #1: DEVELOP A MORNING ROUTINE

As I've talked to people about busyness, I've learned that most people begin their days with Hurry, Worry, and Scurry. They hit the snooze button several times then finally get up at the last possible minute. They chug some coffee and jump in the shower. They throw on clothes and get the kids ready for school, then rush out the door and speed to work. Mornings like this cause your sympathetic nervous system to go into overdrive, to inundate your body with adrenaline and cortisol.

The first few minutes of your day sets the tone for the rest of your day. If you're going to *live* each day with Purpose, Productivity, and Peace, then you must *begin* each day with Purpose, Productivity, and Peace. The instrument for beginning your day well is a morning routine.

In recent years, the topic of morning routines has become popular. Many books and bloggers cover the topic, and several online courses have emerged. Before discussions of morning routines became prolific, I had implemented several iterations that changed based on the season of life. I've loved morning routines for a long time because I am a natural morning person.

There are a few common myths about morning routines.

Myth 1. Your routine should take several hours.

One of my favorite productivity authors has a three-hour morning routine. This lengthy time investment works for him because he doesn't have kids at home and is a successful entrepreneur who can choose his hours.

A three-hour morning routine would require me to wake up at 3 am to still have time to help my kids get ready for school! Don't believe this myth. Your morning routine can take as little as ten minutes.

Myth 2. Your morning routine should focus on productivity.

Most of the material I've seen about developing a morning routine focuses on becoming more productive. There is nothing wrong with productivity. However, you are most purposeful and Productive when you start with Peace.

Myth 3. Your morning routine should be regimented.

Many morning routine proponents believe that you should have a military-like precision to your morning routine. One author has you block out the exact amount of time you'll spend on each activity: read for fifteen minutes, meditate for ten minutes, etc. This methodology works for some people, but I've seen limited success with it.

These three myths about morning routines led me to create a method for developing a morning routine that starts each day with Purpose, Productivity, and Peace.

1. Build a buffet of peaceful activities.

Identify five to ten activities you find peaceful. Think of these activities as your buffet. You can eat any of them, but you don't need to eat all of them.

When you wake up in the morning, depending on how much time you have, select which buffet items you want. The key is that you find these activities peaceful.

My buffet includes:

- Drinking a glass of water (I do this every day to rehydrate.)

- Sipping on a cup of coffee (I do this every day because coffee makes life better.)

- Reading the Bible

- Reading an inspirational book

- Meditating

- Sitting in silence

- Listening to music

- Journaling

- Exercising

I don't do all these activities every morning. Instead, they are my buffet of options. When I wake up, I select a few of the items from the buffet based on how I'm feeling at the moment. Each morning begins with some of my favorite activities, which creates a sense of Peace.

One note about exercising: exercising might not seem like a peaceful activity, but I've found that just a little bit of exercise can help me feel energized instead of stressed. I will often do twenty jumping jacks and pushups to get my blood flowing and save the harder workout for later. Exercise helps clear sleep-fog.

2. Add purposeful and productive options.

Once I've started the day with Peace, I add some purposeful and productive options. Here's my buffet of purposeful and productive options:

- Reviewing my life purpose statement by saying it out loud

- Going through each of my roles and affirmations

- Praying through my day

- Looking over my Dreams and Priorities.

- Reviewing my Top Three Priorities for the week

- Planning my Top Three Priorities for the day

3. Give yourself Margin.

Your morning routine doesn't have to take three hours, but give yourself at least a few minutes for your mind and body to wake up from sleep.

To do that, give yourself some margin. If you only want to spend ten minutes on your morning routine, wake up at least five minutes before that.

4. Start your morning routine at bedtime.

Your morning routine begins before you go to bed. You want to set yourself up mentally and physically for a purposeful, productive, and peaceful morning routine.

Prepare anything you'll need for your morning before you go to bed. Make a glass of water. Have your coffeemaker set to brew. Pull out your workout clothes. This groundwork allows you to transition into your morning routine seamlessly.

To prepare mentally, guard your thoughts before you go to bed. You'll find that you usually wake up in the same mood as when you fell asleep. Use the last minutes before you doze off in gratitude for what has happened and excitement for what is coming, and you'll wake up the same way.

Habit #2: Tame Your Transitions

William Bridges, one of the modern experts on organizational change management, made the point that organizations don't struggle with change. They struggle with the *transition* from where they are to where they are going. It's easy to believe where you are going is better than where you are, but the transitions are hard. He writes, "It's not the changes that do you in. It's the transitions."[44]

Bridges' maxim rings true not only for organizations but also for individuals. Transitions are challenging, yet you encounter them dozens of times every day.

You experience a transition whenever you (a) switch from one activity to another or (b) switch from one role to another.

Here are a few of the transitions you go through every day:

- From sleeping to awake

- From being at home to getting ready for work

- From being a boss at work to being a parent at home

- From the house being quiet to the kids arriving back at home

- From working on a report to your co-worker interrupting you

- From one meeting to another

- From talking to a person to looking at your phone

- From preparing dinner to eating it

- From eating dinner to cleaning up

- From being awake to getting ready for bed

Transitions are inevitable, but they are also trouble. Why?

- Every time you transition, you must refocus your attention. One University of California, Irvine study found that it takes an average of twenty-three minutes and fifteen seconds to refocus after you're interrupted.[45]

- Every time you transition, you stop doing one thing and start doing something else. It takes more time and energy to get the ball rolling on something new.

- Every time you transition, you introduce a bit of stress into your life. When you experience multiple transitions in short periods of time, that stress adds up and causes your sympathetic nervous system to kick in.

Even though transitions are inevitable, you can make them easier to deal with by taming your transitions. When Dorothy and I celebrated our first anniversary, we bought a puppy. (P.S. Don't make that mistake!) When we brought her home, our puppy became the master of our house. She barked all night, chewed our shoes, and demanded constant attention. We had to come home from work at lunch to take care of her. The dog was our master.

These behaviors continued until we tamed her. We had to train her how to be part of our lives. When we tamed her, we became her master.

Transitions are like a puppy. If you let them, transitions will rule (and often ruin) your day. But tame your transitions, and you become their master.

What needs to happen for you to tame your transitions?

1. Minimize your interruptions.

To start, get rid of as many interruptions as you can. If you're talking to a friend, turn your phone on silent. This simple action keeps you from transitioning your attention from your friend to your screen and back to your friend. Turn off email notifications from your computer and devices. Close your internet browser when you need to give focused attention to a project.

If you work in an office, communicate "office hours" that you are available for conversations with your coworkers. But, during non-office hours, ask them to interrupt you only for emergencies.

2. Batch work together.

One of the best ways to tame your transitions is by batching similar kinds of work together. You can do this in several ways:

- Batch all your meetings so that they take place in one day.

- Block specific times in your calendar to respond to email.

- Set aside a couple of hours to do all your administrative work.

- Prepare multiple meals at one time and freeze a few of them.

When you batch tasks together you minimize transitions and maximize your time, energy, and attention.

3. Create Intentional Transitions.

One of the biggest challenges that Oliver faced was adapting from work to home. He worked hard all day, using up a tremendous amount of energy. He would then rush home, making any last-minute work calls on his way. As he walked in the door, he usually had several other concerns that were on his mind, but his family wanted his attention. Sometimes, he had to turn around immediately to go to one of his kids' activities. He told me that coming home felt like walking into a tornado.

We worked together to create an **Intentional Transition** for him. Here's what it looked like:

- He set a reminder to notify him when it was fifteen minutes before the end of the workday.

- He would finish what he was working on, shut down his computer, and clean up his desk. This gave him a sense of closure to the work day.

- On the way home, he completely disengaged from work. He would either sit in silence or listen to music, which allowed him to rest his mind and have some time to himself.

- When he pulled in his neighborhood, he prayed for his wife and kids.

- When he got to his driveway, he put on a big smile.

By the time he got home, Oliver had mentally shifted from work to home. He was reenergized and ready for the evening together. With a few new habits, Oliver created an Intentional Transition and minimized his stress. He became the master of his transitions rather than letting them rule his day.

By minimizing your interruptions, batching your work together, and creating Intentional Transitions, you can stop letting your transitions rule your day.

HABIT #3: BUILD SYSTEMS

One final (un)busy habit is building systems of any repeated actions that you do. If 45% of your life is a habit, many of your daily actions are not only repetitive, but you could maximize them for efficiency and effectiveness. That's where building systems can help.

You already developed a system in this chapter when you designed your morning routine. You're taking a common occurrence (waking up) and designing steps that save stress, time, and energy.

A system occurs when you take your repeated projects and design a series of repeated actions or habits that save you stress, time, energy, and money. Do you see the acronym?

S – Save
Y – You
S – Stress
T – Time
E – Energy, and
M - Money

In my twenties, early in my career, I made a mistake that I thought would cost me my job or my marriage. Over the course of a year, I lost over $6,000 in work-related receipts, and all the expenses were on my personal credit card. I had no records to turn in for reimbursement!

I hated tracking expenses. Compared to the grand and noble work of leadership like shaping a vision, this task bored me. Plus, expense tracking took too long. I usually spent three hours filling out an expense report. My attitude and inability demonstrates my lack of skillset when it comes to administration.

I had to go to my boss and tell him my mistake. He was far more gracious than I deserved. However, it took me about seventy hours to go through the last year of credit card statements and identify every work purchase. I then had to create expense reports for each month's worth of lost receipts.

That's the experience that convinced me I needed a system for reimbursements. Up until that point, I had balked at using systems. The idea of them felt stifling. But after wasting seventy hours to do something that should have only taken a few hours, I decided to try out systems. Since then, I've discovered the power of systems for many areas of life.

You have repeated actions that you do every day, from getting dressed in the morning to checking your email to planning a business trip. Each of those can be systematized.

How do you develop a system? There are six steps. (In other words, there's a system for creating a system!) For most systems, I use Todoist, my project and task management software, but you can do this in a word processor or write it down on paper.[46]

1. Identify the starting and ending points for the system.

When does the system that you're implementing begin and end? When I did this for expense reports, I realized that I had been thinking about them all wrong. I used to believe expense reports began when I started filling one out. In reality, new expense reports began the moment I turned in the old ones. That's when I needed to make sure I was collecting receipts and documenting expenses.

I used to think that they ended when I submitted the report. But, in reality, they didn't end until I received the reimbursement.

2. Identify every step—in order—that occurs between the starting and ending point.

When I did this for expense reports, I discovered thirty-four steps that needed to take place. No wonder I struggled. I was keeping all those steps trapped in my head!

You want to write down every single step, no matter how small. For expense reports, one of my steps was "Open Microsoft Excel."

If you have steps that other people need to do, document those as well. I wrote down steps like: "Email boss for approval and attach expense sheet" and "Receive reimbursement in the mail."

3. Document important notes for the steps.

I wrote down exactly where the file was located on my computer and created a hyperlink so I could get to it. I wrote down the email address for the person I would send the expense report to and even created a template for an email.

The point in this step is taking away any opportunity for confusion or delay. Document everything you need to do.

4. Use the system.

Now for the fun part. You use the system. The first thing I did whenever I filled out an expense report was open my task manager and start working through the system. Systems don't do you any good if you document them and then fail to use them.

5. Tweak the system.

When I created the first expense report system, I identified the thirty-four steps that I needed to follow. As I've gotten better at it and as technology has improved, I've been able to cut it down to eighteen steps. It used to take me three hours to fill out an expense report. It takes about twenty minutes now. Having a system has saved me significant stress, time, energy, and money! It's given me more time to focus on my biggest Dreams and highest Priorities.

After you've experienced the benefits of your first system, you'll want to create systems for other areas of your life. What are some of the projects that you do regularly that you could capture in a system? Here are a few I've found most helpful:

- Travel packing list
- Checking and responding to email
- Yearly lawn care cycle
- Booking travel details for business trips
- Household chores
- Preparing for a presentation
- Writing a blog post
- Decorating for Christmas
- Preparing the house before vacation

Systems are one of the most powerful habits I've found to help live with greater Purpose, Productivity, and Peace. Start by developing one system and implementing it. As it saves you stress, time, energy, and money, you'll add more.

STEP 4: GET BUSY GETTIN' (UN)BUSY

The Develop step helps you learn new ways of living that will prevent you from falling back into busyness, but this step isn't just about introducing new hacks. You'll Develop a (un)Busy calendar, mindset, and habits that will help you live with greater Purpose, Productivity, and Peace.

DEVELOP AN (UN)BUSY CALENDAR

Managing your calendar and time are never the cause of busyness. That's why we've ignored it up to this point. Now it's time to learn new practices that will help you get and stay (un)busy.

- ☐ Change the way you think about your calendar. It's a tool for proactively organizing your life for Purpose, Productivity, and Peace.

- ☐ Time-block your Core 4, Priorities, and boundaries first.

- ☐ Manage your Margin by giving yourself Space between appointments and room for the unexpected.

- ☐ Block out one day every week to stop all work and take a Sabbath.

DEVELOP AN (UN)BUSY MIND

Busyness assaults your mind, causing you to lose focus, get distracted, and allow constant interruptions into your life. A few practices can help you develop an (un)busy mind.

☐ Develop the practice of writing everything down. Take a note-taking tool with you everywhere and write your ideas and actions down as soon as you have them.

☐ Spend ten minutes every day processing what you wrote down.

☐ Accept your (un)Movable Constraints. Determine what you can do rather than saying "if only."

☐ Time-block and practice Daily and Weekly Reflection and Preflection to ensure that your highest Priorities become reality.

DEVELOP (UN)BUSY HABITS

Habits comprise nearly 40-45% of your life. Make (un)busyness part of your life by following three habits: (1) developing a morning routine, (2) taming your transitions, and (3) building systems.

☐ Implement your morning routine so that each day starts with Purpose, Productivity, and Peace.

☐ Determine which regular transitions you experience that cause stress, and Develop strategies for minimizing your interruptions and batching your work together.

☐ Develop Intentional Transitions that help you prepare for potentially stressful transitions.

☐ Determine one system you can Develop and follow the process for building a system.

STEP 5

DRAW OTHERS IN

When I first discovered the process of Gettin' (un)Busy, I only had four steps. Then I worked with Kim.

She had completed Decide, Deconstruct, Design and Develop. I was celebrating with her and telling her how proud I was of her hard work. She told me about experiencing greater Purpose, Productivity, and Peace in her life.

That's when I noticed the look on her face. It didn't last for long, but she looked sad, even defeated. Even though defeat starts with a *D*, I certainly didn't want people to add that feeling to their Gettin' (un)Busy experience.

When I asked what was wrong, she said, "I'm so proud of the work I've done. I (un)busied my life. I know what my biggest Dreams and highest Priorities are, and I'm taking steps every day toward those. But now I feel so lonely."

Those were not the words I expected to hear. Relationships is one of the pillars of The Core 4. I asked her what was causing this loneliness.

"My friends don't understand my new way of life. My family sees the change in me, but it's still strange to them. My coworkers have heard me talk about Gettin' (un)Busy. But they're so hurried, worried, and scurried that they don't understand. I feel all by myself. What in the world should I do?"

She and I developed a plan to help her talk to her family, friends, and coworkers, but much more happened in that conversation. I realized that there was a fifth step to Gettin' (un)Busy—Draw Others In. We'll concentrate on Drawing In three groups: your family, your friends, and your team at work.

16

DRAW IN YOUR FAMILY

It can feel lonely if you're the only person in your family who has committed to Gettin' (un)Busy and no one understands you. Fortunately, there are ways that you can help your family understand what you've experienced. More importantly, you can draw them into a life of Purpose, Productivity, and Peace with you. Here are a few hints that can help you with your immediate family, specifically your kids.

1. Embrace your authority as a parent.

As the parent, realize that you have the authority to change the way that your family lives. I've talked to a lot of parents who feel helpless and trapped by their kids' activities. They tell me that they feel like unpaid taxi drivers.

As parents, we may convince ourselves that we are making these sacrifices in our children's best interests, but in reality, kids aren't feeling any better than we are about all these commitments. As I noted earlier, the average level of anxiety among today's high school student is higher than that of someone who would have been institutionalized for anxiety in the 1950s![47] The primary cause of this anxiety is overcommitment and putting too much pressure on themselves to perform everything with excellence.

Stuart Brown writes:

"We may think we are preparing our kids for the future when we organize all their time, when we continually ferry them from one adult-organized, adult-regulated activity to another. And, of course, to some degree, these activities do promote culturally approved behavior as well as reinforce our roles as good parents. But, in fact, we may be taking from them the time they need to discover for themselves their most vital talents and knowledge. We may be depriving them of access to an inner motivation for an activity that will later blossom into a motive force for life."[48]

You, as the parent, have the ability and authority to guide your family to live at an (un)busy Pace. You can determine the number of activities your kids do. You can regulate how many nights your family will participate in activities. You are not helpless! You have the ability—in fact, the responsibility—to lead your family to live at a sustainable Pace.

Embrace your authority to lead your family to live with Purpose, Productivity, and Peace.

2. Overcommunicate your commitment to Gettin' (un)Busy to your kids.

Let your kids know that you have chosen to live at a different Pace than others. You don't want to make a sudden change and not explain to them the reasons why.

Don't think of communication as a one-time event. Communication around Gettin' (un)Busy can take place every time someone in the family *has an opportunity to take on a new commitment*. Help your kids evaluate whether they want to take it on. Help them think about the family's capacity and whether this commitment will exceed that capacity. Help them determine if they need to drop a current activity in order to make room for a new one.

You can also communicate by *celebrating the times that you (un)commit and when you decide to say* no *to a commitment.*

Whatever you celebrate gets repeated. So, celebrate the times when your family makes choices toward (un)busyness.

3. Choose together over to-do.

In our busy society, "family time" no longer means quality time. Parents schedule play dates for young kids and then "watch" them participate while looking at their phones. Older children stay in school all day then scarf down a fast food meal in between football practice, community service, and piano lessons. Parents spend hours every week transporting children to various activities and complain that they feel like taxi drivers.

When families choose together over to-do, they spend more quality time with the people they love most.

Here are a few ways to choose together over to-do:

1. (un)Commit from the (un)necessary.

One Inhibiting Belief will drive your family to busyness faster than others: thinking of your family as isolated individuals rather than a single-functioning unit.

For a few years, the Henderson family struggled with this Inhibiting Belief. They thought they owed it to their three kids to treat them fairly by always allowing each one to pick an activity. John played lacrosse; Lilly danced; Esther participated in theater productions.

Not only did the Hendersons allow each child to choose one activity, but the parents also expected each child to do well in school, take weekly piano lessons and attend Bible studies. Before they knew it, every evening was packed with multiple commitments.

The Hendersons made the mistake of thinking of their family as isolated individuals. Each child had the capacity to meet all of their own obligations. But, as a family, it was all too much. They rarely had dinner together and almost never had a weekend at home. In spite of the fact that the parents made sacrifices of time and money to provide these opportunities, the children complained about feeling exhausted and overwhelmed.

When you think about your family as a single-functioning unit, you choose activities by evaluating your *family's* capacity rather than each individual's capacity. Here's how you do this:

- **Identify your (un)commitments.**
  Many parents fear that they are depriving their children when they limit their activities. On the contrary, excessive, organized activities deprive children of creativity, leadership skills, mentoring opportunities, conflict management skills, and health.[49] Isn't it better for children to learn compromise, collaboration, and how to live in mutually supportive community than to have their own self-interests catered to all the time? Use the *Commit to (un)Commit Worksheet* in Chapter 9 to identify each of the obligations your family has and evaluate your feelings about each one. (un)Commit from as much as you can. The health of the family unit requires self-sacrifice from both parents and children.

- **Build boundaries for family-only time.**
  You may want to set aside an evening each week or day on the weekend for the family to simply be together.

- **Reevaluate your plans every ninety days.**
  Family capacity is seasonal. For example, the Hendersons knew that lacrosse required John to attend multiple practices each week from February to June. During that season, Lilly cut back to one dance class per week and Esther took a hiatus from theater, prepping to try out for the fall production instead. At the end of lacrosse season, they created a new plan for their commitments.

- **Determine pockets of (un)activity.**
  Find stretches of time in which your family doesn't participate in anything. The Hendersons allocated summer break as a "no commitment zone." They did not sign up for any clubs or camps. They ate dinner together most nights and spent time playing games or reading in the evenings. They limited the number of nights that anyone could be away from home.

Choose together over to-do. It will look differently for every family, but you make it possible when you (un)commit from the (un)necessary.

2. Eat intentional dinners together.

The benefits of families having dinner together have long been proven.[50] The good news is that the average American family has dinner together nearly five nights each week.[51] The bad news is that the average dinnertime today lasts less than twelve minutes, down from ninety minutes in 1959.[52] To make matters worse, when families eat together, it's common for each person to stay transfixed on their smartphones.

Make it a priority to not only eat together but also to put away your devices, turn off the TV, and talk to each other. Ask everyone to share what they're grateful for. Or have everyone tell the best and worst parts of their days. By planning intentional dinners, you "trade accumulation and activity for conversation and community."[53]

3. Find activities to do together.

Even in togetherness, it's vital to children's development that they discover things they love to do. The best way to demonstrate the family's support is by finding ways of participating in those activities together. Here are some things I've seen work:

- Take family karate lessons.

- Take turns choosing a movie to watch together instead of letting each person have their own screen.

- If one of you has a special event such as a recital, game, or award ceremony, make sure everyone in your family attends.

- Ask your kid who loves the piano to teach the other ones how to play simple songs.

- After soccer practice, have everyone in your family hang out on the field and kick the ball around.

Help your family get (un)busy by choosing together over to-do.

4. Set aside family Core 4 time.

Schedule regular time with your family for Relationships, Recreation, Rest, or Reflection. Make this time sacred to your family so nothing can interrupt it. Here are a few ideas:

- Establish a weekly game night. Let your kids invite other friends to participate, but don't allow your kids to go out.

- Set media-free times during which no one can use a computer or technological device.

- End each week with family Reflection and Preflection. Reflect on the previous week and talk about the upcoming week. This discussion will ensure that everyone is on the same page.

Success at Gettin' (un)Busy isn't just about you. It's about your family also. Your family needs you to raise the next generation to get (un)busy so that they don't fall into the same trap that you did. These steps will help you Draw In your family.

17

DRAW IN YOUR FRIENDS

S everal years ago, Dorothy and I invited a family from our church over for dinner, Josh, Amber, and their two girls. We didn't know them well, and we wanted to get to know them better.

We grilled out and ate on our porch while our kids played together. After dinner, we walked down to our backyard firepit and roasted s'mores. We sat around the fire for several hours getting to know each other.

A few months after that dinner, Josh shared with us how uneasy they felt coming to our house. He told me that, on their way to dinner, they were speculating about why we had invited them over. People don't have time just to "have people for dinner" anymore. They guessed we had an agenda or wanted to talk about something they had done to displease us.

On the way home from that dinner, Josh asked Amber, "What do you think they wanted from us?"

Amber responded, "I think they just wanted to get to know us."

"Yeah, that's what I think," Josh responded. "Kinda weird, huh?"

Getting to know them was, in fact, our agenda. Since then, Josh and Amber have become dear friends, and we've laughed many times about their disbelief that someone wanted time with them just for the pure sake of enjoyment.

We're quick to believe everyone wants something from us or is selling something. It's easy for others to become distrustful when you want to develop a relationship with them. Besides, people are so busy that it's hard for them to make time for relationships.

So how can you draw friends into an (un)busy life?

1. Own the loneliness.

Have you ever experienced the soreness in your muscles after a great workout? It's uncomfortable. It's also confirmation that you worked out very hard and pushed yourself.

The same is true with loneliness.

When you've done the hard work of Gettin' (un)Busy, you will probably feel some loneliness in the beginning. Other people haven't yet caught up to you. You have more Space in your life than they do. The way you're living might not make much sense to them.

The loneliness is confirmation that you've killed busyness. It's the soreness you experience after working hard to free yourself from the epidemic that is hurting so many people.

Own this loneliness. Acknowledge that you feel it. Accept the discomfort. You won't be here alone for too long. Wear your loneliness as a badge of honor. You have gotten (un)busy!

2. Accept others' pace; invite them into your pace.

One of the effects of busyness has been the creation of one-hour friendships. Before busyness became so prevalent, people would spend slow time with friends. Dinners would last multiple hours. Even having coffee with a friend could take a long time.

Busy people only have time for one-hour friendships. Here's what a one-hour friendship may look like: You meet a friend for coffee. They rush in—maybe even late. They spill out an update, mainly on how busy their life has been. Then, they look at their watch and say, "Sorry, I've gotta go. I need to…." From start to finish, you had one hour together.

As you look to Draw In your friends into an (un)busy life, accept their Pace, but invite them into yours. Accepting their Pace means not expressing frustration with them for their busy lives. It wasn't that long ago that this was your Pace of life as well.

Instead of expressing frustration, invite them into your Pace of life. When you schedule time with them, block ninety minutes instead of sixty. Help them slow down by modeling a slower Pace of life. When they talk about their busyness, talk about how you decreased your stress, overwhelm, and exhaustion. Talk about Relationships and Recreation that you're enjoying.

When they say, "Wow! That must be nice!" let them know that they can experience it, too.

3. Talk about the benefits before the process.

If you tell people that you've worked to get (un)busy, they'll be hesitant to listen to you. Remember, busyness is based in the Inhibiting Beliefs that you need to be more, do more, and get more. If you start by telling people you've been Gettin' (un)Busy, it may scare them. They'll think you're attacking the core of their significance.

Instead, tell them about the benefits you've experienced—identifying your Dreams, turning those into Priorities, and becoming more productive. Tell them about the time you've gotten back into your schedule, the reduction in your stress, and the increase in your energy.

As you begin to talk about the benefits that you've experienced, some of them will ask you how it happened, which opens the door to talk about the process of Gettin' (un)Busy.

Also, allow me to help. Give them a copy of this book. Start a discussion group. Join the online course together at **www.gettinunbusybook.com/course**.

Relationships are hard when your friends are overcommitted. Lead the way and draw them into your (un)busy life. It's one of the greatest gifts that you can give to them. Help them escape stress, overwhelm, and exhaustion.

It's also one of the greatest gifts that you can give yourself. You're blessing yourself by getting your friends' time and attention.

At first, they'll think that you're "kinda weird" for Gettin' (un)Busy. But give it some time. Your friends will love (un)busyness, and your relationships will flourish.

18

DRAW IN YOUR TEAM

I've spent most of my adult life as a student and practitioner of leadership. I discovered early in my career how vital leadership is to success and learned that *as the leader goes, so goes the team.*

Much of my passion for helping people like you get (un)busy stems from my passion for leadership. I discovered the dangers of busyness because I saw the toll it took on my personal life and my life as a leader. I realized the busier I became, the busier my team and organization became. My busyness affected everyone I influenced.

However, when I began the process of gettin' (un)busy, my new way of thinking and living influenced the people I worked with. I noticed that, as a team, we were slowing down. We weren't as hurried, worried, and scurried. But, more than that, we achieved bigger team goals. We had more time for our families and somehow, we worked less and accomplished more.

WHY LEADERS MUST (UN)BUSY THEIR TEAMS

If you lead a team, you want that team to show up every day at their best. You want them to be passionate about your goals. You want them to work hard to achieve them. And you probably want to have fun along the way.

But your busyness will prevent all of that from happening. If the people on your team are addicted to busyness (like you were), they won't show up every day at their best. They'll be drained on every level. They won't be passionate about your organization's goals; they'll be overwhelmed by them.

You certainly won't have fun along the way because it's hard to have fun when you're stressed, exhausted, and over-whelmed. It's hard to enjoy your work when you resent it. After you go through the journey of Gettin' (un)Busy, then it's time to lead your team through it as well.

Oliver did this for his team. When he first came to me for help, he had moved up his organization's ladder and was now overseeing nine direct reports and had over 300 people who were part of his department. Before he worked to get (un)busy, it seemed like everyone in his department was stressed, exhausted, and overwhelmed all the time.

As Oliver started living with Peace, it overflowed into his direct reports. His direct reports started influencing their direct reports. Within a few months, the culture of his entire department had changed.

The department as a whole felt a sense of Purpose, Productivity, and Peace. They worked hard but they didn't feel exhausted every day. They worked fewer hours than they ever had before, yet they accomplished more of their Priorities. The change in this one department benefited the rest of the organization.

It all started with Oliver deciding to get (un)busy. You see, as the leader goes, so goes the team.

Whether you're an entry-level leader, a middle manager in a large corporation or the CEO of a Fortune 500 company, if you decide to get (un)busy, it will affect everyone you lead and it will improve your team's performance and productivity.

How to Get Your Team (un)Busy

How can you lead your team to get (un)busy? Here are a few ways that I've found most helpful.

1. Talk about busyness.

As a leader, what you talk about matters to your people. They need to hear what you're learning and how you're growing.

Tell your team what you've learned about busyness. Share with them the effects of busyness on their lives as individuals. Tell them about the effects on organizations. Apologize to them for any busyness that you modeled to them and let them know you want to create a team that lives with Purpose, Productivity, and Peace.

Leaders need to value both results and relationships. When you express care and concern for the people you lead, they will follow you because they sense that you value them as individuals.

Talk to your team about busyness, and let them know that you're ready to get (un)busy as a team.

2. Set and communicate clear boundaries.

The first way to start getting your team (un)busy is to set clear team boundaries around time, communication, and travel.

Time Boundaries. When I examine the average organization, I find a subtle mentality permeating the current culture. The mentality is, *We work until we finish the job.* On the surface, it appears that this mentality would reinforce responsibility and hard work. But that mentality does significant damage to people and organizations. There are two problems with that mindset:

(1) Parkinson's Law (once again) reminds us that work expands to fill the time allotted. Therefore, if you don't

set a boundary on the hours that a person works, the work will keep expanding to fill every available minute.

(2) The job is never finished. There have been some days when I've checked everything off my list for the day. But in over twenty years of work, I've never gotten to the end of the day and thought, *I finished everything I could possibly do. I'm not sure what I'm going to work on tomorrow.*

These two problems reveal why it's important to set time-boundaries. Put a cap on the number of hours that a person can work each week, even for salaried employees. Research has shown that productivity declines significantly after fifty hours of work.[54] Some companies are even experimenting with 32-hour work weeks that increase job engagement and work-life balance.[55] You'll be amazed at how much people can accomplish when you limit their hours.

Communication Boundaries. In a hyper-connected world, communication creates overwhelm. At a recent workshop, Michael, one of the participants, came up to me afterward to talk about his team. They were in the habit of texting each other about projects throughout the night. He was receiving notifications as late as 2 am. Everyone felt pressure to respond to the texts no matter the time, and they were all exhausted.

The irony is that Michael oversaw this team. He felt obligated to reply to every text message to set the example of hard work.

I helped him quickly create communication boundaries around the *type* of communication and the *hours* of communication.

(1) Type of Communication. Michael determined that *texting* was for emergencies only. *Email* was for communication with outside clients. *Instant Messaging* was for internal communication. They used a program called Slack.

(2) Hours of Communication. He set the boundary that no one needed to respond to communication after 6:00 pm or before 8:00 am. If it was an emergency, they would text the word EMERGENCY followed by a phone call.

These simple adjustments in expectations led to an almost overnight change in the behavior of the team. Michael experienced a full night's sleep for the first time in years!

Help your team create communication boundaries by developing and reinforcing guidelines around the types and hours of communication.

Travel Boundaries. If your team has members who frequently travel, give them time back when they return. They've sacrificed time away from family and home responsibilities. Allow them some of their time back.

A friend of mine recently traveled for five days with his job. He left Monday morning and didn't return home until late Friday evening. He missed multiple nights with his family, but he was expected to be back in the office first thing on Monday morning. That's a recipe for burnout and disengagement.

Contrast this with another friend of mine who spends 65% of her working time on the road. Her boss allows her to take extra-long weekends and longer vacations. She keeps a record of how much time she spends on her travel. Then, when she wants to take extra time away, she shows her boss and gets approval.

Help your team build strong boundaries around work by setting them and communicating those boundaries to your team.

3. Minimize your team's goals.

According to *The 4 Disciplines of Execution*, when a team has two or three goals, they have a 90% chance of achieving those goals with excellence. When a team has more than that, they begin to falter. If they have four to ten goals, they will only achieve one or two of them. However, if they have eleven or more goals, they will likely accomplish none of them. That's right. Zero.[56]

Despite this compelling research, most organizations that I see still select a huge number of goals to focus on at any time. The problem is that no individual or team can focus on that many goals simultaneously.

If you want to help your team get (un)busy and become more productive, minimize the number of goals that you work on at one time. Reducing goals is one of the hard jobs of leaders. Purge most of the goals you *could* do so you can focus on the two or three that you *must* do.

4. Use the SIMM framework.

Most of the time when leaders identify goals, they add them on top of already stretched teams. These teams are overextended and then have those goals piled on top of them.

Whenever I help teams identify their top two or three goals, I then take them through a SIMM exercise. Here's what happens.

(1) Once you have identified your goals, take stock of everything else your team does. Look at all the activities, reports, meetings, and products you're involved in.

(2) Evaluate everything through the **SIMM** framework: **S**top, **I**nitiate, **M**aintain, **M**aximize.

S—What needs to Stop? What are you doing that you no longer need to do? What can you stop doing that will give you more time to focus on your goals?

I—What do you need to Initiate? When you identify new goals, it leads to new projects and work. But these initiatives take significant time and energy. So, minimize the number of new initiatives that start at any one time. It is better to launch one or two initiatives that have a high likelihood of success than dozens of new projects that will likely falter.

M—What do you need to Maintain? As you look at your goals, what areas are "good enough?" By leaving these things as they are, you create more time for your initiated goals.

M—What do you need to Maximize? Some of your commitments need upgrades to accomplish your goals. What needs to improve to move forward?

These four questions help you stop piling on more work. Instead, they keep your team focused on what's most important.

Your Leadership Matters

As a leader, Gettin' (un)Busy isn't just a personal decision. There is no such thing as a personal decision for you. Every decision you make affects other people. Everything you do affects other people. It doesn't just affect the people who report directly to you. It affects their friends and family. It also affects people who report to them and all *their* friends and family.

Your leadership matters because you can bless people or curse them—you make their lives better or worse. When you lead your team to busyness, you're cursing them. You're leading them and their families to stress, overwhelm, and exhaustion.

However, when you lead your team to Purpose, Productivity, and Peace, you'll bless them and their families. And you'll accomplish more than you did when you were all stressed, exhausted, and overwhelmed.

So, get (un)busy. Not only in your life but also in the lives of your team.

STEP 5: GET BUSY GETTIN' (UN)BUSY

You've gone through all the steps of getting yourself (un)busy, but, if you don't get others around you involved, (un)busyness can be lonely. Draw your family, friends, and teammates into Gettin' (un)Busy.

DRAW IN YOUR FAMILY

You want to draw your family into (un)busyness so that you can choose Purpose, Productivity, and Peace together.

- ☐ Embrace your authority as a parent.
- ☐ Overcommunicate your commitment to Gettin' (un) Busy to your kids.
- ☐ Choose together over to do.
- ☐ Set aside Family Core 4 time and don't allow anything to interrupt it.

DRAW IN YOUR FRIENDS

At first, your friends may think that your (un)busyness and high priority on relationships are weird. But you can help them embrace (un)busyness with you.

- ☐ Own the loneliness.
- ☐ Accept others' Pace, but invite them into your Pace.
- ☐ Talk about the benefits of (un)busyness before you talk about the process. Share your Dreams and Priorities and your reduction of stress, overwhelm, and exhaustion.

☐ Invite them to get (un)busy together. Buy them a copy of this book, join the online course together.

DRAW IN YOUR TEAM

As the leader goes, so goes the team. When you get (un)busy, you can help your team and all those they influence do the same. Gettin' (un)Busy will make your team more productive.

☐ Talk about busyness with your team.

☐ Set and communicate clear work boundaries around time, communication, and travel.

☐ Minimize your team's goals so that you only have two or three at a time.

☐ Implement the SIMM framework for evaluating what needs to Stop, Initiate, Maintain, and Maximize.

EPILOG

You did it! I believed in you the whole time, even if you doubted yourself. I know that you weren't designed to lose your life to busyness. Now, you've done it. You've gotten (un)busy!

You Decided that busyness wasn't worth the price and that you were going to get (un)busy.

You Deconstructed Inhibiting Beliefs, Bad Habits, and (un)Wanted Commitments.

You Designed Pace, Space, and The Core 4 into your life. You even Designed your Dreams and Priorities.

You Developed the an (un)busy calendar, mindset, and habits to increase your Purpose, Productivity, and Peace.

You Drew Others Into your (un)busy way of life and are influencing them.

So, what's next? There are two final actions that I want you to take.

1. PLAN A CELEBRATION

I believe that you will look back on this experience of Gettin' (un)Busy as one of the defining moments in your life. In the time it took you to read this book and implement the actions, you've gone from stress, overwhelm, and exhaustion to Purpose, Productivity, and Peace. You've moved from Inhibiting Beliefs to Empowering Truths. You've shifted from living out other people's Dreams and Priorities to discovering your own and making them happen.

Your accomplishment is worthy of celebration.

Gather your family and invite friends over. Share your achievement and celebrate together.

I'd like to celebrate your hard work as well. Email me at garland@advanceleadership.live and tell me your story.

There's also a second action to do. **It's time to get busy.**

2. GET BUSY.

Wait. What?!?

I know what you're thinking. "I just spent all this time Gettin' (un)Busy…and now you're telling me to get busy? Make up your mind!"

Let me explain.

One of my favorite movies is *The Shawshank Redemption*. It tells the story of Andy, a man who was imprisoned for a crime he didn't commit. Andy strikes up a great friendship with another prisoner, Red.

At one point in the movie, Andy tells Red about his dreams once he gets out of prison. Andy wants to move to Zihuantanejo in Mexico, have a boat on the Pacific Ocean, build a hotel, and enjoy his life.

Red, on the other hand, believes he couldn't survive on the outside. He's been in prison for so long he had been "institutionalized."

As Andy describes his dreams, Red says, "I don't think you ought to be doing this to yourself, Andy. I mean, Mexico is way the hell down there. And you're in here. And that's the way it is."

Andy agrees. "Yeah, that's the way it is. It's down there, and I'm in here. But I guess it comes down to a simple choice: **Get busy living. Or get busy dying.**"

That's your choice now, too. But now you know the irony of that statement. *Only when you live without busyness can you get busy living.*

Live the life of your Dreams and Priorities. Replace stress, overwhelm, and exhaustion with Purpose, Productivity, and Peace. Enjoy the life you have. Get busy living. Or get busy dying.

YOUR STORY

At the time of this writing, it's been seven years since my appointment with Dr. Tate. Ten years since he told me that he was concerned for my life.

I rarely get headaches. My heart palpitations are gone. I have increased energy.

More importantly, I've been able to fulfill many of my Dreams:

- I led my team to get (un)busy.

- I finished my doctorate.

- I got in better shape.

- I left a job that stifled my creativity and passion.

- I helped one of my best friends grow his company.

- I moved my family to our Dream location.

- I started a company with my wife that helps overwhelmed influencers live and lead with greater Purpose, Productivity, and Peace.

- I consulted with dozens of companies to help them accomplish their organization's highest priorities.

- I published my first book.

I accomplished all of that while working less hours and enjoying life more. More importantly, I have more time with my family and friends than ever before. I got busy living.

I can't wait to see what's next for me.

But I also can't wait to see what's next for you. One of my priorities is to help you accomplish your priorities. So, I want to hear from you. Email me at garland@advanceleadership.live to tell me how your life has changed.

I don't know what's next for you, but I do know this much. You got (un)busy, so get busy living!

ENDNOTES

1 Kahn, Herman, Anthony J. Wiener, and Hudson Institute. *The Year 2000; a Framework for Speculation on the Next Thirty-Three Years*. New York, Macmillan, 1967, 197.

2 Saad, Lydia. "The "40-Hour" Workweek Is Actually Longer--by Seven Hours." *The Gallup Blog*, August 29, 2014. Accessed April 10, 2015. http://www.gallup.com/poll/175286/ hour-workweek-actually-longer-seven-hours.aspx.

3 Benson, Herbert. "Are You Working Too Hard." *Harvard Business Review OnPoint* Spring 2015 (2005), 64.

4 Weale, Sally. "Do You Often Feel Ill on Holiday..." *The Guardian*, November 26, 2002. Accessed November 18. 2018. https://www.theguardian.com/lifeandstyle/2002/ nov/26/healthandwellbeing.health.

5 Pang, Alex Soojung-Kim. *Rest: Why You Get More Done When You Work Less*. New York: Basic Books, 2016, 26.

6 *Rest,* 26.

7 Leahy, Dr. Robert L. "How Big a Problem Is Anxiety?" *Psychology Today*, April 30, 2008. Accessed November 18, 2018. https://www.psychologytoday.com/us/blog/ anxiety-files/200804/how-big-problem-is-anxiety.

8 Denizet-Lewis, Benoit. "Why Are More American Teenagers Than Ever Suffering from Severe Anxiety?" *The New York Times Magazine*,

October 11, 2017. Accessed December 15, 2017. https://www.nytimes.com/2017/10/11/magazine/why-are-more-american-teenagers-than-ever-suffering-from-severe-anxiety.html.

9   Nutt, Amy Ellis. "Why Kids and Teens May Face Far More Anxiety These Days." *The Washington Post*, May 10, 2018. Accessed October 15, 2018. https://www.washingtonpost.com/news/to-your-health/wp/2018/05/10/why-kids-and-teens-may-face-far-more-anxiety-these-days/?noredirect=on&utm_term=.afd3ee09f753.

10 Kogon, Kory, Adam Merrill, and Leena Rinne. *The 5 Choices: The Path to Extraordinary Productivity*. New York: Simon & Schuster, 2015, 40.

11 " "Remember When Cigarettes Were Good for You?" *Sky News*, February 10, 2015, 2015. Accessed December 10, 2018. https://news.sky.com/story/remember-when-cigarettes-were-good-for-you-10371944.

12 Dobbs, Deborah Walsh. "Rebel against busyness." *Good Life Family* (April 5, 2018. Accessed December 10, 2018. https://goodlifefamilymag.com/2018/04/05/rebel-against-busyness/.

13 Selye, Hans. *The Stress of Life*. Rev. ed. McGraw-Hill Paperbacks. New York: McGraw-Hill, 1978.

14 Compiled from: Hart, Archibald D. The Hidden Link between Adrenalin & Stress: The Exciting New Breakthrough That Helps You Overcome Stress Damage. Waco, Tex.: Word Books, 1986.

Swenson, Richard A. Margin: Restoring Emotional, Physical, Financial, and Time Reserves to Overloaded Lives. Rev. ed. Colorado Springs, CO: NavPress, 2004.

Stanton-Rich, Howard M. and Seppo E. Iso-Ahola. "Burnout and Leisure." *Journal of Applied Psychology* 28, no. 21 (November 1998), 1932-33.

15   Maslach, Christina. *Burnout: The Cost of Caring.*
     Cambridge, MA: Malor Books, 2003.

16   "Burnout and Leisure," 1932-3.

17   *Rest,* 163.

18   Kethledge, Raymond Michael and Michael S. Erwin.
     Lead Yourself First: Inspiring Leadership through Solitude.
     New York: Bloomsbury USA, 2017.

19   McChesney, Chris, Sean Covey, and Jim Huling. *The 4
     Disciplines of Execution: Achieving Your Wildly Important
     Goals.* 1st Free Press hardcover ed. New York: Free
     Press, 2012, 24.

20   Harter, Jim. "Employee Engagement on the Rise
     in the U.S." *Gallup,* 2018. Accessed August 26,
     2018. https://news.gallup.com/poll/241649/
     employee-engagement-rise.aspx.

21   Puzzanghera. "Average Full-Time Workweek
     Is 47 Hours, Gallup Says." *Los Angeles Times,*
     August 28, 2014. Accessed November 1,
     2018. https://www.latimes.com/business/
     la-fi-average-workweek-gallup-labo
     r-day-20140829-story.html.

22   If you want to learn more about how to design
     your company to intentionally create Raving Fans
     intentionally, check out www.swozleadership.com.

23   Webb, Brandon and John David Mann. *Mastering Fear:
     A Navy Seal's Guide.* New York, New York: Portfolio/
     Penguin, 2018, 51.

24   Lyubomirskey, Sonia, Lorie Sousa, and Rene
     Dickerhoof. "The Costs and Benefits of Writing,
     Talking, and Thinking About Life's Triumphs and
     Defeats." *Journal of Personality and Social Psychology* 90,
     no. 4 (2006).

25   Murray, W. H. *The Scottish Himalayan Expedition.*
     London: J.M. Dent & Sons, 1951, 6-7.

26   Kreider, Tim. "The 'Busy' Trap." *New York Times Opinionator*, June 30, 2012. Accessed March 2, 2015. http://opinionator.blogs.nytimes.com/2012/06/30/the-busy-trap/?_r=2.

27   Brown, Brené. "Shame V. Guilt." *brenebrown.com*, 2013. Accessed October 30, 2017. https://brenebrown.com/blog/2013/01/14/shame-v-guilt/.

28   DeGroat, Chuck. *Wholeheartedness: Busyness, Exhaustion, and Healing the Divided Self*. Grand Rapids, Michigan: William B. Eerdmans Publishing Company, 2016, 14-15.

29   Frazee, Randy. Making Room for Life: Trading Chaotic Lifestyles for Connected Relationships. Grand Rapids: Zondervan, 2003, 17.

30   Cross, Gary. "A Right to Be Lazy? Busyness in Retrospective." *Social Research* 72, no. 263-86 (2005), 282, emphasis added.

31   Parkinson, C. Northcote. *Parkinson's Law: The Pursuit of Progress*. London: John Murray, 1958.

32   Brown, Stuart L. and Christopher C. Vaughan. *Play: How It Shapes the Brain, Opens the Imagination, and Invigorates the Soul*. New York: Avery, 2009.

33   Brown, *Play*.

34   "Energy Drink Unit Sales in the United States from 2015 to 2017 (in Millions)." Last modified 2017. Accessed December 1, 2018. https://www.statista.com/statistics/558031/us-energy-drink-unit-sales/.

35   *Rest*, 148.

36   *Rest*, 121.

37   The estimate of the number of daily decisions a person makes varies widely. On the high end, some say that a person makes 35,000 decisions every day. Daum, Kevin. "How to Make Great Decisions (Most of the Time)." *Inc. Online Magazine*, October 16, 2012. Accessed

December 29, 2018. https://www.inc.com/kevin-daum/
how-to-make-great-decisions-most-of-the-time.html.

On the low end, Sheena Iyengar, a Columbia
University decision researcher, says that the average
American makes 70 conscious decisions each
day. Iyengar, Sheena. "How to Make Choosing
Easier." *TEDSalon NY2011*, 2011. Accessed
January 2, 2019. https://www.ted.com/talks/
sheena_iyengar_choosing_what_to_choose/
details?language=en.2018.https://www.ted.com/
talks/sheena_iyengar_choosing_what_to_choose/
transcript?language=en)

38 Achor, Shawn. *The Happiness Advantage: The Seven
Principles of Positive Psychology that Fuel Success and
Performance at Work.* New York: Crown Business, 2010.

39 Moran, Brian and Michael Lennington. *The 12 Week
Year: Get More Done in 12 Weeks Than Others Do in 12
Months.* Hoboken, New Jersey: Wiley, 2013.

40 Although this method is popular, I first discovered it in
The 5 Choices, 85.

41 Barnes, M. Craig. *Searching for Home: Spirituality for
Restless Souls.* Grand Rapids, Mich.: Brazos Press, 2003,
118.

42 Bailey, Chris. *The Productivity Project: Accomplishing
More by Managing Your Time, Attention, and Energy
Better.* First edition. ed. New York: Crown Business,
2016.

43 Fox, Justin. "Habits: Why We Do What We
Do - an Interview with Charles Duhigg." June
2012. Accessed 2018. https://hbr.org/2012/06/
habits-why-we-do-what-we-do.

44 Bridges, William. *Managing Transitions: Making the Most
of Change.* 3rd ed. Philadelphia: Da Capo Press, 2009.

45 Mark, Gloria, Daniela Gudith, and Ulrich Klocke,
"The Cost of Interrupted Work: More Speed and

Stress." Twenty-sixth annual SIGCHI conference on Human factors in computing systems, Florence, Italy, 2008.

46   For a free, two-month trial of Todoist Premium, go to https://todoist.com/r/garland_vance_aukmsy.

47   "How Big a Problem is Anxiety?"

48   *Play,* audiobook.

49   *Making Room for Life*, 96-103.

50   Weinstein, Mariam. *The Surprising Power of Family Meals: How Eating Together Makes Us Smarter, Stronger, Healthier, and Happier.* Hanover: Steerforth, 2006.

51   Delistraty, Cody C. "The Importance of Eating Together." July 18, 2014. Accessed June 28, 2019. https://www.theatlantic.com/health/archive/2014/07/the-importance-of-eating-together/374256/

52   Braider, Jessica. "Family Dinner Statistics. March 30, 2019. Accessed June 28, 2019. https://www.thescramble.com/family-dinner/family-dinner-statistics/

53   *Making Room for Life,* 130.

54   Popomaronis, Tom. "Science Says You Shouldn't Work More than This Number of Hours a Week." May 9, 2016. Accessed May 21, 2019. https://www.inc.com/tom-popomaronis/science-says-you-shouldnt-work-more-than-this-number-of-hours-a-day.html

55   Parkinson, Suzi. "The Ideal Work Week: How Many Hours Should You Work?" August 9, 2018. Accessed May 21, 2019. https://www.gqrgm.com/the-ideal-work-week-how-many-hours-should-you-work/

56   *The 4 Disciplines of Execution*, 24.

THANKS

Dorothy, you are my biggest hero. You dream big and love well. You are a constant encourager and have believed in me more than I believed in myself. Thank you for making everyone you influence and everything you touch better—including being the first editor of my manuscript. Above all, thank you for being true to your name. You are a gift of God. I adore you.

Calvin, Sophie, and Toby, thank you for being three of the most amazing people on the planet. You bring such joy to all those you know, and I am proud to be your father. Thank you for the years of forgiveness and grace as I learned to get (un)busy.

Thank you, Mom, for always being there. Even though you're not here any longer, I still feel your prayers energizing and encouraging me. I miss you.

Dad, thank you for your indefatigable encouragement and belief. You have contributed so much to my life spiritually, mentally, emotionally, and financially. Thanks for saying, "Go, Goo!" when it didn't feel like anyone else would.

Thank you, Tim and Shirley for being such wonderful in-laws. Thank you for your love, encouragement, and support over the last twenty years. And for your daughter!

Thank you, Dr. John Basie and Dr. Craig Carr. As my dissertation readers, you refined my thinking and poured over my words more than you wanted to. I am forever indebted to you both for your investment in my life and ideas.

Thanks to all my fellow researchers, thought leaders, and experts who have shaped me over the years: David Allen, Chris Bailey, Scott Belsky, Peter Bregman, Brené Brown, Stuart Brown, Brendon Burchard, Stephen Covey, Chuck DeGroat, Michael Hyatt, Dan Miller, Brian Moran, Cal Newport, Matt Perman, and Skip Prichard.

Reggie Fenner, thank you for saying two words that changed my life. By the way, I think *you're (un)containable*, too!

Dr. Rich Plass, thank you for speaking life-altering words to our family on two occasions. First, you told me to limit my hours to increase my effectiveness and make friendships my priority. Second, you encouraged Dorothy to turn our crazy dream of moving to Tennessee into a priority. I can't wait to hear what you say to us next time!

Brandy Montambo, you are a rock star because you empower others to become rock stars. Your encouragement and design work increased my determination and provided much-needed energy bursts.

Scott Wozniak, thank you for being a long-time friend and contagious optimist. Your years of camaraderie and accountability still push me to be better.

Kary Oberbrunner, David Branderhorst and the Author Academy Elite Tribe, thank you for your passion for igniting souls and helping people get their messages out to the world. Because you show up filled up, we can, too.

Special thanks to friends who have encouraged me along the way and sought to get (un)busy: John and Virginia Moore, Josh and Amber Hembree, Ben Miller, Ben and Kelly Culbertson, and many friends in Asheville, North Carolina, Rome, Georgia, Katy, Texas, Knoxville, Tennessee and from Carson-Newman University, Beeson Divinity School, and Denver Seminary.

To my clients across the world who have interacted with me for years regarding busyness, Purpose, Productivity, and Peace: Thank you for listening to me, wrestling with me, and implementing the ideas that we discussed. Your lives are a testament to the power of Gettin' (un)Busy.

To the Triune God—Father, Son, and Holy Spirit. Praise to you for being infinitely energetic and never in a hurry. Thank you for making Sabbath before we needed it and helping me discover it long after I needed it. Thank you for moving at a slower pace than I would like and reminding me to slow down so that I can catch up with You.

ABOUT THE AUTHOR

Garland has been helping people and teams get clarity about their life and leadership for over twenty years. He is an author, speaker, and consultant. Along with his wife, Dorothy, he cofounded AdVance Leadership, which helps overwhelmed influencers and organizations live with Purpose, Productivity, and Peace.

Garland also serves as a Senior Consultant with Swoz Leadership, a consulting firm that helps maximize organizations through executive development and creating raving fans.

As a former Leadership Development Pastor and Director of one of Chick-fil-A's nonprofits, Garland has poured into influencers at all levels. He's helped thousands of people discover and live out their life purpose, enhance their clarity and productivity, and impact the world around them.

Garland earned a Doctorate in Leadership and Spiritual Formation from Denver Seminary. There, he researched the effects of busyness on leaders and how to overcome both individual and organizational overcommitment.

As much as he loves to work, it's not his highest priority. Garland enjoys reading, watching movies, drinking coffee, trying new food, engaging in deep conversations, running, and East Tennessee hiking. But most of all, he loves spending time with his wife, Dorothy, and their three children.

Web: AdVanceLeadership.live and gettinunbusybook.com
Twitter: @garlandvance
Facebook: facebook.com/garlandvancepage
LinkedIn: www.linkedin.com/in/garland-vance

YOUR NEXT STEPS WITH GETTIN' (UN)BUSY

NEED MORE **GETTIN' (un)BUSY** ?

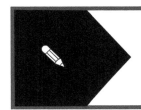

ASSESSMENT
Not sure if you're overcommitted?
Take the assessment to discover your level of busyness and what you can do about it.

TOOLKIT
Get free tools that will help you kill busyness. You will also receive the latest updates about living with Purpose, Productivity, and Peace.

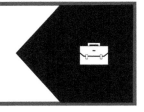

COHORT
Experience the power of an (un)busy community! Receive training videos, group coaching, and get to know like-minded people who want to get (un)busy together.

COACHING
Want more personalized help?
Get one-on-one coaching to help you get (un)stuck and start accomplishing your biggest dreams and highest priorities.

GETTIN' (un)BUSY FOR YOUR ORGANIZATION

Maximize productivity. Minimize stress. Increase profitability.
Bring AdVance Leadership to your organization.

SPEAKING

Inspire your people to get (un)busy and accomplish their highest priorities.

CONSULTING

Empower your leadership team. Design a strategy that guides your company to perform with Purpose, Productivity, and Peace.

WORKSHOPS

Build a new company culture and train your teams to get (un)busy.
Half-day, Full-day and 2-day workshops available.

EXECUTIVE COACHING

Keep you and your leaders on the right track so they can accomplish more and influence others to do the same.

CPSIA information can be obtained
at www.ICGtesting.com
Printed in the USA
LVHW051131070819
626836LV00003B/3/P